574.526

SRUC

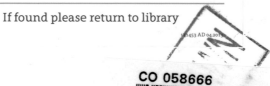

The Woodland Trust Book of
BRITISH WOODLANDS

The Woodland Trust Book of
BRITISH WOODLANDS

Michael Allaby

DAVID & CHARLES
Newton Abbot   London   North Pomfret (Vt)

(*frontispiece*)
A wood that grows on the steep side of a hill is a 'hanger'. Gilbert White spent many hours studying the wildlife of just such a hanger as this, and his description of it, in *The Natural History of Selborne*, has been a source of delight for country-lovers for almost two centuries. This is not his hanger – but maybe some modern Gilbert White is at work there now, preparing to delight future generations! This one is on the South Downs; it comprises a splendid stand of beech trees with an understorey of yew (*M. Nimmo/Frank Lane Agency*)

British Library Cataloguing in Publication Data

Allaby, Michael
    The Woodland Trust book of British woodlands.
    1. Forests and forestry—Great Britain
    I. Title
    941'.009'52   SD179

ISBN 0-7153-8572-0

Drawings by Rosemary Wise
Text © Michael Allaby 1986
Drawings © David & Charles 1986

Typeset by Typesetters (Birmingham) Ltd,
Smethwick, West Midlands
and printed in Great Britain
by Butler & Tanner Limited, Frome and London
for David & Charles (Publishers) Limited
Brunel House Newton Abbot Devon

Published in the United States of America
by David & Charles Inc
North Pomfret Vermont 05053 USA

Contents

1
The Woodlands of Britain

When I was a small boy I lived in Ashbourne, in Derbyshire. You could get a bus to take you the five miles into Dovedale, along steep, twisting roads, the hedgerows mere inches from the side of the bus, and the smells swirling in through the open windows of summer. It was an exciting ride, because the driver always tried to knock a few minutes off the official journey time to allow himself a cup of tea and a smoke between trips. In any case he had to go fast down the hills if his ancient bus was to make it up the other side. Sometimes he misjudged it and we had to get out and walk the last few yards to the top.

Dovedale was not inside a National Park in those days, just a place for family picnics. There was Thorpe Cloud to climb, and the icy-cold clear Dove, with stepping stones from which I contrived to fall many times. You could drink the river water, although it was forbidden by parents to do so. It was a family place, crowded even then, in the early years of the Second World War, but only by local people; those from each small town or village occupied their own special patch. There was resentment if someone from another community 'stole' your favourite spot.

We boys did not visit Dovedale much by ourselves. The bus fare deterred us, and Bradley Wood attracted us. We were not supposed to go there, for fear of child-stealing gypsies, and Bradley. No child was ever stolen, and I never found out who Bradley was, or whether he really existed at all. He was a legendary figure, at least ten feet tall and armed to the teeth, who might leap from behind a tree at any moment. He added spice to our visits and no one, real or imaginary, can ask for more than that. We did no harm, of course. We did not even pick the bluebells because, much as we liked them, they would have been evidence of our trespass, and we knew perfectly well that they wilt before you get them home. Generations

7

of children have known, loved, and risked punishment to visit Bradley Wood.

When I was older we moved, and I acquired a bicycle which increased my range dramatically. The Wyre Forest was now within reach; I remember it as a place of brambles, difficult of access, appropriately surrounded by barbed wire, where I narrowly missed stepping on a wasps' nest. More recently I have camped in the Forest of Dean with my own family, and walked through tiny fractions of its large wooded area. These days I walk in Cornish woods on warm summer evenings after work, to breathe the scented air and purge the crowding words from my head.

Woodlands, you see, feature at particular points in my life, and I am not unique. They are part of the lives of nearly all of us, and always have been. They are part of our history, but more important, they are part of our personal memories. Our love of woodland is not new, although if you think of the vivid descriptions of woods that occur in folk tales, it seems that our attitudes to it are different. In the stories the woodcutter and his family are always honest but desperately, grindingly poor. The forest is a place of some danger, the haunt of evil witches, goblins and other malign spirits, of fierce animals and of brigands. Now we look more kindly on our woodlands and no longer find them threatening. Perhaps our attitudes really have changed, but the change occurred long ago; those tales are of great antiquity, the outside historical events and costumes of their characters being updated as required.

At one time, woodland was not a good place in which to live. Indeed, few people have ever done so; it is difficult to earn a living there – even the woodcutter was poor – and you cannot grow food crops. In early times criminals sought refuge in woodlands and preyed on travellers passing through. To simple, rather super-stitious people, the tall trees, the shade, the ample cover that might conceal danger, combined with a mild attack of claustrophobia to permeate the wood with malevolent spirits. Fierce animals were there then, true, but the threat from them was much exaggerated. Bears and boar will not attack humans except in self-defence, and even wolves kill habitually only for food, and they do not eat humans. British woodlands have never harboured venomous rep-tiles or invertebrates, at least not since humans have been here.

Times and attitudes change. When songs and stories came to be composed about him, Robin Hood, a fairy-tale character possibly based on a real person who lived in a particular historical period, was a hero, not a villain. That was long after he had died, if he ever lived. Even if he was real his forest was a fiction: most of Sherwood

Woodland that occurs naturally, rather than as a plantation, has no sharp edges. It extends fingers into the adjoining land, and there may be gaps, with only isolated trees, separating the main wooded area from smaller woods nearby. The woodland is allowed to blend unobtrusively into the landscape, and the length of the woodland edge is increased. This is of great ecological value because the 'ecotone' area, where woodland merges into open country, provides habitats for some woodland species, some species of the open countryside, and some species peculiar to the woodland edge itself, thus making it very rich in wildlife. This wood, on the chalk downs of Hampshire, consists of yew and whitebeam with hawthorn (*N. Nimmo/Frank Lane Agency*)

Forest was heathland by his time. The malevolence that lurked in the forest lurked there far earlier than this – probably back in the days of the Celts – and the soldiers who preyed on the peasants are more likely to have been Roman than Norman. By Norman times the conservation of woodlands was becoming fashionable, although Norman game-laws were much harsher than the Saxon laws they replaced.

Long ago, Britain was blanketed by forest that had developed slowly as the glaciers retreated. People entered the country to hunt the large game that fed on the abundant vegetation growing in the nutrient-rich meltwaters of the tundra, ahead of the extending tree line. As they learned to domesticate herbivorous animals, and to till the ground and grow cereal crops, they began to clear the forest, working hard and effectively with their stone axes and fire. The major forest clearance happened early; it may well have been more or less complete by the time the Romans departed. Many people suppose that medieval Britain was a landscape of forest, with clearings for farm land. It was not so. In fact there was not much more woodland then than there is now. According to the Domesday record, there were few places where you could travel more than about four miles in a straight line through woodland; you would leave the trees and encounter a village, with farms around it. The towns and cities were small, but the countryside was populated as densely then as now, and the demand for food from a farming system that was much less productive than ours required that almost all suitable land should be pressed into service.

Some time after the Romans had gone, in the so-called Dark Ages, people must have started to realise that it made more sense to manage woodland and live off its income, as it were, than to use up the capital by continued clearance. By the Middle Ages many landowners were conserving their woodlands, and learning how to manage them. The British valued such woods as remained to them, and were coming to regard each loss as a matter for critical comment. Those of us who would conserve woodland today belong to an old, honourable and very British tradition.

Neither the building of the Royal Navy and merchant fleets, nor even the smelting of iron in the early years of the Industrial Revolution, had much effect on the area of woodland. After that first, ancient clearance it remained largely unchanged until very recently. In the last thirty or forty years, however, we have embarked on a new woodland clearance, comparable in extent to that of our Celtic ancestors, but with only the woodland area left to us by them remaining to be cleared. Obviously we shall not remove every last wood, but many are going, and the conservation task is urgent.

Figures describing the total area of tree cover are misleading, for they include the large areas of plantation forest that have been established during this century. Plantation forest is quite different in its composition and its ecology from natural or semi-natural forest, which comprises mainly native or at least long-naturalised species. This is as true of broadleaved plantations as it is of the conifer plantations so despised by many lovers of the countryside.

In this book I try to tell something of the story of British

Because commercial forestry is not allowed to use more valuable farm land, plantations are forced on to marginal land, often on high ground, where trees must be grown close together to shelter one another. These intrusive, sharp-edged, solid blocks of dark green conifers contrast starkly with the softer browns and greens of the hillside and with the grey rocks above, and detract from the natural beauty of the landscape. This is part of Beddgelert Forest, in Wales (*W. Broadhurst/Frank Lane Agency*)

Norway spruce, with recent plantings in the foreground and more mature trees in the background. While the conifers are young a rich variety of herbs, shrubs and even a few small trees grow among them, providing a wide range of foods for wildlife, and ample shelter. This area, near Wendover, Buckinghamshire, supports a population of firecrests (*Regulus ignicapillus*), a small bird very like a goldcrest. Unfortunately, the habitat will change radically as the spruce trees grow, and will change yet again when the time comes to fell them, for all the conifers in the block are of the same age, and will mature together (*Leo Batten/Frank Lane Agency*)

woodland, beginning where that story really begins, in a past that may seem remote to us now, but that in geological terms is recent. Beginning with the ice ages, and the interglacials that separate them, we come to our present interglacial. I describe some of our individual woodland trees, and the types of woodland they form, discuss the ecology of woodland and its management, and look at the difference between woodland management and forestry.

The British countryside is to be visited, seen and enjoyed, and no book can provide a substitute for direct experience. That is why the latter part of this book gives a directory of woodlands, arranged geographically, in alphabetical order of counties or regions. Each of them illustrates some point made in the text. Most of them are open to the public; visit them. When you have read the book and seen some of these woods, and of course any others near your home area, you may be persuaded of the need to conserve such woodland as we have, and to plant more. Britain already has a smaller wooded area than most European countries – only some 9 per cent of the land area is wooded. In Japan, the country with which Britain is often compared, the figure is 60 per cent. We cannot aim so high, but we could do far better than we are doing now.

The book, then, aims to encourage the love of woodlands by showing the part they have played in our history and their value to us and our remaining wildlife today. It has been written with the close collaboration of the voluntary organisation most concerned with the conservation of woods, the Woodland Trust.

I have received much help and advice from Elizabeth Hamilton, Deputy Director of the Trust, and from John D. James, the Trust's Director, and it is they who gathered the information from which the directory has been compiled. Without their assistance the book would have been much poorer, and I am grateful to them. However, although the book appears under the name of the Trust and with its blessing, it is I who have written it: if it contains errors they are mine, and the opinions it expresses are also mine, not necessarily those of the Trust. Usually we agree; where I know our views diverge I have said so and put both opinions. Ailsa, my wife, also provided valuable help, with research especially into the palaeo-ecology of Britain, and with the task of indexing. Without her help the book would have been weaker. It would also have taken longer.

We play for high stakes. If we lose and still more of our woodlands disappear, Britain will be impoverished. If we succeed, then for generations to come there will be Bradley Woods in which children may play, and adults roam, and begin to experience the half-wild, half-natural countryside which is theirs, and to which they belong.

2
Woodland Walks

 A walk in woodland at any time of year will offer something to see, something new that was not there last time or was hidden. Each season has its own special quality, but there is a particular magic about an autumn morning. When the sun is low in the sky, so its yellowing light enters the wood obliquely, to disperse only slowly the thin mist which formed around the still recent dawn, and the air is still, sharp with the threat of frosts which have yet to harden the ground. There is a clarity of perception: it is shared by early spring, but you will not find it in quiescent winter, nor at the height of the dark, luxuriant summer.

This clarity is no figment of fancy. More light penetrates to the ground when the leaf-fall has opened the canopy, and more of the ground is illuminated when the sun is low in the sky than when it is high. This is a matter of simple geometry – you can demonstrate it with an electric torch. Shine it vertically downward and it will light a more or less circular disc. Shine it obliquely and it will light a much larger elliptically shaped area. That is not the only apparent paradox. There is more light when the sky is overcast than when the sun shines brightly. This is because clouds scatter light, so it enters the wood from many different angles. If you doubt this, measure it with a photographic light-meter.

The illumination is not so intense, but it is enough for you to see more of the woodland floor than you would in other seasons. In spring it is enough for the flowers which rush to complete their flowering and seed formation before the trees and the climbing sun have time to shade them. In a broadleaved wood, it is summer which is the dark time.

As children we are taught to think of autumn as the season which heralds the ending of the year. We have to count our years from some point, of course, because we have an obsession with measuring things, but plants and animals do not share our passion for marking

The entrance to Wormley Wood, Hertfordshire, which is owned by the Woodland Trust. It covers 138 hectares (340 acres) and scientifically is of national importance because almost all of it is ancient, making it the largest oak-hornbeam woodland still remaining in its semi-natural state. There are paths and rides, which visitors are welcome to walk along (*Sterling Photographics/The Woodland Trust*)

the passage of the days. If the preparation of a meal begins with the collection of the ingredients, then for them the autumn, a time of preparation, marks the beginning of a new year. The work of the old year is done. Flowers have flowered, seeds have been dispersed, young have been born, raised or died, and (among most small animals) left their parents. Migrant birds have gone. Invertebrate animals have completed their reproduction. It is time to clear away, start afresh, and prepare for the next phase in the eternal cycle.

True, that preparation must include the finding of secure places, and perhaps provisions, to survive the winter, for in our high latitude success or failure for many a plant or animal turns on its ability to endure the cold, hunger and, when water freezes, thirst of January. Preparations must be completed before the quiet time of deep winter, when everything rests; and rest, too, is a form of preparation for the frenetic activity that must begin in the spring.

Sometimes the preparations within a wood in autumn can be observed. Many animals prepare mainly by eating voraciously. Look at the resident birds, the common ones we take for granted like thrushes, blackbirds and starlings, which still inhabit the woods, their original home, when they are not congregating in our cities. In autumn they are sleek, and so obese that at times you wonder they can fly at all. They have laid down a thick layer of fat that will sustain them when food is scarce. The starling, which used to be called more poetically the 'calling-bird', is scorned, but it is handsome and in autumn it is acquiring its densely spotted winter plumage. Many birds change their plumage with the seasons, but the starling has the distinction of altering the colour of its bill, which in winter is dark and in spring will turn bright yellow.

You may look for evidence of wood mice and bank voles, for they leave behind them the remains of their meals. They both like rose-hips, but for different reasons: the mice eat the seeds and discard the flesh, but the voles eat the flesh and leave the seeds. It is not too easy to find the tiny rose seeds, but the remains of a hip from which the seeds have been taken are a sure indication that a mouse has had a meal.

You can tell whether the mice and voles are feeding without looking for abandoned hips, though. Look at the briars themselves, while there are still some hips on them. Notice the way the hips are attached and look for similar structures where the hips are missing. Small rodents detach the hips with a sharp, clean bite, so stalks that have been bitten through indicate their presence nearby. If most of the hips have gone you can be sure there are many of them. In the far north, when the days shorten until there are only eight hours of

16

Autumn fruits

daylight, voles store food. In most of England, though, the days are too long to trigger this behaviour, even in midwinter.

The size of a small mammal population is usually calculated from the numbers caught by trapping (which does not injure the animals, but should not be attempted by anyone without proper equipment, the guidance of an experienced zoologist, and a very good reason). If the traps suggest there are few mice and voles, but the briars are being stripped, an ecologist would suspect that either the traps are in the wrong places, or the small rodents are 'trap-shy'. Ecologists are creatures of habit and tend to work over the same sites again and again. As they do so, trapping and releasing small animals as they go, some mice and voles learn that a trap contains food and dry bedding, and that release will follow a meal and a sleep, so they enter a trap whenever they find one. Others learn to fear capture, and being handled by a human, and avoid traps. Trapping alone is never a reliable guide to their numbers, and the briars supply valuable clues. This is especially important because the size of a

Badger emerging from sett

population varies widely from place to place and from time to time. You can expect to find up to 30 bank voles in an acre of woodland in autumn, depending on the amount of food available, but in late spring there could be as few as 5. Autumn is a good time for vole-watching! It is an even better time for mouse-watching, because in autumn an acre of woodland may contain up to 40, falling to less than 1 an acre in spring.

It is not so much the harsh conditions of winter that reduce populations as the large spring migrations, as animals which spent the winter in sheltered quarters move on to find new sources of food. Small rodents lead short lives in any case. The average life expectancy for a wood mouse is a mere 17 weeks and for a bank vole only 10 to 12 (although some individuals may live for much longer and voles have been known to live for as long as 18 months). So animals which live through the winter are likely to die in the spring, because by then they are old.

Larger mammals leave more evidence. Badgers, for example, patrol their ranges by well-trodden paths of their own, from which they make only small deviations. Where the wood slopes steeply upward from the path you may see what looks like a slide, or the mark made by dragging a heavy object, leaving the wood, and you may find a tunnel made through dense vegetation to one side of the path, about large enough to allow the passage of a terrier-sized dog.

Probably this is a badger route, but it is worth pausing for confirmation. Look for hairs caught on the twigs to the side of the path, or above it. The long, coarse, grey hairs of a badger are as unmistakable as its face. If the hairs are reddish-brown, the path has been used by a fox.

The entrance to a badger sett is like the entrance to a rabbit burrow, but larger, into the side of a bank, and usually marked by a mound of earth, excavated, thrown outside, and left. Rabbits can make large burrow entrances, but a badger tunnel is at least 8in in diameter, and is likely to be much wider than this at the entrance. The earth outside it often contains old bedding – hay, bracken, or other plant material – which you will not find outside a rabbit burrow. An entrance that is much too large to have been made by rabbits, but which has no plant material in the heap of earth nearby, is probably the burrow, or earth, of a fox.

Badger droppings may be found not at the entrance to the sett, but close by in a shallow open trench. A trench containing what might be mistaken for dog droppings does not necessarily indicate that you are close to a sett, for badgers have latrines in various places, probably used to mark the boundaries of their ranges. If there are no rabbit droppings, look for more entrances to the sett nearby, and if the ground is soft, look for large footprints in which the long claws are clearly visible. Those are badger prints. If you do find a badger sett you will also know that this part of the wood is well drained, and the ground fairly dry, for badgers do not like their homes to be damp.

If you are walking in woodland in Hertfordshire, Buckinghamshire or Bedfordshire in early autumn, it is just possible that you may see an animal which looks much like a grey squirrel, but is about half the size and has a much bushier tail. You may find it further afield if local rumours are to be believed; the stories are not entirely incredible, for the animal is attractive, used to human company, and may well have been captured and transported to new places. It is the fat, or edible, dormouse (*Glis glis*). The Romans rated edible dormice highly as a delicacy, feeding them in beech and oak woods, then imprisoning them inside a jar and fattening them on currants and chestnuts. They probably brought their dormice to Britain, but those which live here today can claim no such distinguished ancestry: they were released at Tring Park in 1902 by Lord Rothschild. When they are not scampering about our woodlands, mainly at night but sometimes by day, they climb into attics to feed on stored apples, making a great deal of noise about it; local councils are sometimes called to evict them. Unfortunately, they also strip bark from trees and can do considerable damage in the woods they inhabit.

Dormice hibernate, and the edible dormouse hibernates for about seven months of the year. It is famed for its ability to sleep – the Germans know it as *Siebenschläfer*, the 'seven-sleeper'. True hibernation among mammals is less common than many people suppose. Squirrels, for example, do not hibernate: indeed they cannot survive for more than a few days without food. You see them in autumn gathering food they will store and then forget.

A common mammal that really does hibernate, is the hedgehog. It lives near the edges of woodland and leaves few signs of its presence. Its footprints are easily mistaken for those of a rat, and although its droppings are distinctive, they are small. The best way to see hedgehogs is to visit the wood soon after dark with a powerful torch.

An animal that is to hibernate must lay down body-fat to act as a store of food, for its metabolism does not cease, and it continues to require 'fuel'. The hedgehog feels sleepy when the air temperature falls, and as it loses consciousness its body temperature falls from 34°C to that of the surroundings, the best temperature for hibernating being around 4°C. Its heart slows from 190 beats a minute to about 20, and its respiration to about 10 breaths a minute. Clever enough, but the problems have only begun.

Whenever an animal uses food, by altering its chemical composition it creates waste. As the hibernating animal cannot eliminate the waste from its body, it must be stored, including waste products which could be very poisonous, such as excess salts. Animal bodies, including our own and those of our relatives the hedgehogs, lose water fairly readily, partly in urine, mainly through respiration and perspiration, but they retain salts. We need to drink in order to dilute the salts and keep constant the salt concentration in our bodies. An animal cannot drink while it is hibernating, but some loss of water continues because it still respires; so it must have ways to maintain a constant salt balance. Its body does this by extracting salts and storing them in complete isolation until the animal awakens and can excrete them. It is this physiological trick which is the really clever one, and the need for it

If a broadleaved tree is cut close to ground level without disturbing the roots, most species – there are exceptions – respond by producing many shoots, each of which will grow into a new stem. This is coppicing, and far from injuring trees it tends to prolong their lives. It also produces a very characteristic kind of woodland, with dense clumps of shoots growing very straight, and separated by open spaces that allow herbs to thrive. This is an ash coppice in Kent (*M. Nimmo/Frank Lane Agency*)

that allows us to dismiss as nonsense any idea of humans hibernating.

Before hedgehogs hibernate they build nests beneath vegetation, or sometimes inside rabbit burrows. They usually build several nests each, and in the course of the winter may wake and move several times. In early autumn it is the adult males which are preparing to hibernate. Later it is the females, and the young hibernate later still, the youngest last of all. (It may be as well to keep this information from the children when discussing bedtime!) Of course, never disturb a hibernating hedgehog.

On a pale autumn morning you can see the structure of the woodland, as though its skeleton had been stripped. As the leaves fall, the denser parts of the wood become visible. You can tell by their size the relative ages of the trees, whether young trees are establishing themselves to replace those which die or are felled, and if trees have been managed, by coppicing or pollarding. This shows more clearly when the trees are bare than when they are in full leaf and might be mistaken for shrubs. It is a good time to survey a wood.

You may have noticed in our own woodlands, or even in aerial pictures of exotic forests in other parts of the world, that all the tallest trees are almost exactly the same height. Trees need sunlight, and the more sunlight they can obtain the more strongly they will grow. It pays them, therefore, to be as tall as they can. The tree which can grow taller than its neighbour wins more light, and that is to its advantage – but there is a drawback. Trees also need moisture. They take this from the soil and pump it upward to the growing tips of their twigs, and to their leaves. If those delicate tips are dried out, they will cease to grow. As soon as a tree stands higher than those close to it its growing points are exposed to the desiccating wind, and its growth is stopped. Try as it may, it cannot much exceed the height of the other trees in the stand. There are exceptions, giants which have grown so exuberantly as to overcome the check, but they are not common. Every tree would gain more light by being taller than the other trees, but because of the wind above the tree-tops, very few achieve their aim. They end up all the same height.

For the same reason, when you can see trees silhouetted against the skyline their tops often indicate the direction of the prevailing wind, appearing to have bent with it. They are not actually bending; the tips have been dried out and prevented from growing on the most exposed side, but the stunted twigs have sheltered those downwind of them, which have grown larger. This cannot make the top of the tree slope, for the twig which grows upward and out of its shelter will be dried. Instead there is more lateral top growth on the downwind side. Since the branches are longer on one side of the tree than the other, but the top of the tree is level, the effect is to make the tree seem to bend with the wind.

Once the leaves have fallen some people find it more difficult to identify tree species – the naming of things is an obsession of ours. But that is not really true; certainly you can identify the composition of the wood, even if you do not positively identify each individual tree. With a little practice, the outer bark of a tree, its shape and way of growth, help in identification. But my point is that the leaves have not vanished: they are on the ground, around your feet, and much easier to reach than when they grew high above your head. Whatever may be going on above the tree tops, deep inside the wood the wind can never blow strongly, and leaves are not likely to travel very far, except perhaps along wide straight rides. If you find the leaves of a particular species in abundance to one side of the path, then you cannot be far away from the tree to which they belonged. The leaves beside the path, and which crunch beneath your feet, are now yellow, red or brown, but no harder to identify for that. It is by their shape they are distinguished, not by their colour. The crunching of leaves is an evocative sound, at least for me. I still hear and feel the leaves through which I loved to walk as a child, going unhurried to and from school during the term which led at a snail's pace to Christmas. These days, like so many sober citizens, I never go out of my way to crunch through piles of leaves if anyone is looking.

Not all the leaves fall, of course. Broadleaved trees are not necessarily deciduous – nor conifers necessarily evergreen. There are exceptions on both sides of the gymnosperm-angiosperm divide, and it is not that which distinguishes the two groups, but their method of reproduction. All the same, broadleaved evergreen trees are not so common in Britain as they are in lower latitudes. The shedding of leaves is a means of preparing for a shortage of water, for in high latitudes – no matter how it may appear to us – the trees regard winter as a dry season. They need water in its liquid form, so snow which lies around the base of the trunk, or frozen puddles, do not count. When the temperature falls below freezing point, conditions are dry. It seems strange to state that polar regions, where most of the land is buried deep beneath ice and snow, is extremely arid, but unless liquid water is available, arid is what it is. If healthy leaves are present, water is being supplied to them: it rises through the trunk, passes along the branches, into the twigs, and so to the leaves. It is 'pumped', but the pump is simple. Water

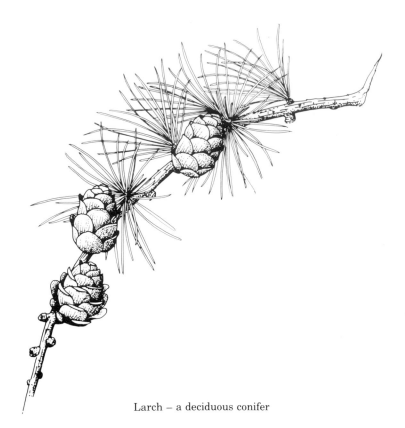

Larch – a deciduous conifer

evaporates from the surface of the leaves, and escapes into the
atmosphere, through stomata or pores. This causes a loss of
pressure in the tiny vessels in the leaves, and water enters from
below to fill it. It is this pressure, in fact the pressure of the
atmosphere, which lifts water through the plant. If the leaves
remained in place through the winter, they would continue to lose
water which in this dry season might be irreplaceable. That would
cause severe damage to the tissues in the woody parts of the tree,
and the tree itself might not survive. It is to forestall this that the
deciduous tree withdraws nutrients from its leaves, and then
detaches them.

It is the withdrawal of nutrients which causes the leaves to
change colour. Leaves are green because their cells contain
chlorophyll, of which most varieties (there are several) are green; in
most species that dominates all other colours. In autumn the
chemical changes that take place in the leaves include the breaking-
down of chlorophyll. As it is destroyed it loses its colour and other
pigments, yellow, red and brown, replace it. It is the leaf-fall which
gives us the colours of autumn. We used to label the season by its

most obvious natural feature, the fall; North Americans have retained the name.

The fall of the leaves is a preparation not only for winter, for it brings other advantages. Like anything else, leaves grow old and worn, and less efficient at their main task of manufacturing sugars. Evergreen trees shed their leaves too, as you will know if you have picked up lawn clippings close to a holly tree; but they do not shed them in a particular season, just one or two at a time as the need arises. Deciduous trees are able to make a fresh start each spring, and this means that when they are needed most urgently, all their leaves face the warming sun while they are young and in mint condition.

Deciduous trees are not alone in their need to conserve water during the winter. All trees face the same problem, but the evergreens approach it differently. They have tough, waxy leaves, through whose surface water passes more reluctantly. Many conifers have leaves that are reduced to needles, as in the pines, spruces and larches, or to very narrow blades, like those of yews and some firs, or to the tiny, scale-like leaflets of cedars and cypresses. The surface area of such leaves is reduced to a minimum; that, and the waxy outer surface, reduces water loss. It is strange to think of the British climate as dry, especially in winter, but it is to seasonal aridity that the trees have adapted. Is the glory of autumn diminished by the knowledge that it is all the result of preparations for imminent drought? I think not.

If the trees have been left undisturbed, and the air is clean, they may be festooned with lichens, glistening from the leafless branches with water droplets condensed out of the mist. The stark stems and branches and the traceries of lichens hanging from them give the wood a strange ethereal quality said to be found in the cloud forests of tropical mountains. Identification of lichens is a skilled business; there are believed to be almost 1,400 British species. Their classification is complicated by the fact that a lichen is formed from the symbiotic partnership of an alga and a fungus, the fungus usually determining the overall appearance of the lichen. The alga manufactures carbohydrates by photosynthesis, and nourishes the fungus. So lichens are now considered to be fungi with an unusual way of obtaining the nutrients they need. Those which hang from trees are most likely to belong to the genus *Usnea*, or at least to the family Usneaceae. They repay detailed study, if you can get to them – they do tend to hang inaccessibly from trees on steep slopes or high out of reach. If you are prepared to learn the unfamiliar and forbidding dialect of biological English in which they are described, and have a good lens with which to admire the beauty of their fine structure, a study of them will carry you deep into the miniature world they inhabit. The woodland will be seen to contain worlds within worlds – growing ever smaller. The lichens themselves, and the mosses with which many of them associate, emerge as the trees of a new forest, with its own populations of plants and animals. If you can find a copy, the best book I know on the subject is *Introduction to British Lichens* by U.K. Duncan (published by T. Buncle & Co Ltd, Arbroath). Apart from giving full descriptions of all the more common species, Dr Duncan gives useful information on how to collect specimens, how to prepare them for examination at home, and how to examine them.

Some lichens are versatile, but most have definite preferences as to the substance (the 'substrate') on which they grow. Some *Arthonia* species, for example, most of which grow on bark, prefer their bark to be smooth, so you often find them on birch; *Usnea hirta* prefers pine. In general, broadleaved tree species support many more lichens than conifers do. Lichens require moist air, and are much commoner on the western side of the country than in the drier east. They are very common indeed in the narrow sheltered valleys of Cornwall, where the luxuriance of the plant life is another indicator of a humid climate. Summer visitors who pass through the valleys on their journeys to and from the beaches, and feel cheated when their enjoyment is spoiled by wet days, forget that the inland scenery that delights them would be less attractive were it not for the high rainfall. Lichens are very sensitive to the air around them, and are used widely as indicators of air pollution. But it does not follow automatically that a heavily polluted area will support no lichens, or that the presence of lichens indicates clean air. It is more complicated than that. Two species of *Lecanora*, one species of *Candelariella*, and probably other lichens as well, can grow abundantly in air containing the sulphur dioxide other lichens find intolerable. A lichenologist can recognise these species, but they may confuse anyone who is not expert. The absence of competition from other lichens may encourage them to grow prolifically, and some of them seem actually to prefer polluted air.

Uncritical acceptance of the role of lichens as indicators of air pollution has been called into question over the matter of 'acid rain'. Pollution caused mainly by sulphur dioxide and oxides of nitrogen, emitted mainly by power stations, was said to be causing serious damage to lakes in Scandinavia and to conifer forests in Germany, where claims were made that very many trees were dead or dying. Yet visiting scientists found the forests supporting lichens in abundance, including species which are known to be intolerant of sulphur dioxide, although clearly some trees were suffering. The matter is being studied intensively and it will be some time before anyone can be sure what is happening. For the time being scientists have formed a tentative conclusion that 'acid rain' is not directly harmful because the acid is far too dilute. Damage can be caused by dry gases and solid particles that are deposited on leaves, but only at concentrations higher than those occurring at present. The sulphur-sensitive lichens survive because the levels of atmospheric sulphur dioxide, and acids formed from sulphur dioxide in the air and in clouds, are very low. The damage to German trees may be due not to the sulphur compounds alone, but to the combined effects of sulphur compounds, nitrogen compounds and ozone, the principal source of the pollution being road traffic in Germany itself, combined with harsh weather conditions. Although the acids washed down in the rain are too dilute to cause direct damage, they may acidify soils and fresh water that contain little calcium or other neutralising agents. This can injure plants, especially those for which the soil is already as acid as they can tolerate. It can also affect fresh water and so harm aquatic life. It may explain why many Scandinavian lakes are being affected, while the forests surrounding the lakes remain unharmed. Some British lakes and rivers are suffering too, but so far as anyone knows our woodlands are not. The world is more difficult to understand than those who seek instant remedies may suppose, and instant remedies rarely work.

Lichens make a wood look ancient, but the antiquity is in the mind of the beholder. The lichen cannot be older than the tree on which it grows, although lichens develop slowly so that the young tree they colonise may be mature by the time they are clearly visible. When the tree dies and falls the lichen falls with it, and its offspring move to a new sapling.

It is not only the lichens which fall. So do the ferns you may see growing where branches join the main stem of a large tree. Usually they are the common polypody, but any plant which produces only small roots, used mainly for anchorage, can grow as well on a tree as on the ground, if the tree provides purchase and a small depression in which water may collect. A plant which grows in this way is an 'epiphyte', using its host only for support and taking no nutrients from it. It does no harm to the tree. In his book *Discovering the Countryside; Woodland Walks*, David Bellamy noted that the popular Victorian hobby of collecting ferns to be grown at home depleted Epping Forest of its epiphytes; but if you move further from areas densely populated by voracious collectors, the ferns are still

27

common enough, and even in Epping Forest they may return. So, I fear, may the popularity of the hobby.

It is not only fern collectors who devour the products of the woodland. Collectors of wild flowers have done some damage in the past; fortunately wild plants usually return. Today many are protected by law. According to the Wildlife and Countryside Act 1981, Part I, Section 13, any unauthorised person who intentionally uproots any wild plant is guilty of an offence. An authorised person means the landowner or someone acting with the permission of the landowner. The law does not forbid you to weed your garden, but it does stop you from robbing the countryside. If a plant is included in the schedule of 62 protected plants included in the Act, it is an offence to pick it even if you do not uproot it, or even to collect its seed. The message is clear enough: do not pick wild flowers.

The autumn woodland boasts no carpets of bluebells, but a few campion may still provide spots of pink, and low on the ground, almost hidden, here and there you may find dog violets or pansies, still in flower or flowering for a second time. Our best-loved flowers, ancestors of many which we cultivate in our gardens, grow most naturally in woodland. The foxgloves now stand flowerless, brown and breaking, their seeds spilling among the nettles in preparation for the rise in temperature that will bring a new generation of those striking trumpet flowers, marked as guidepaths for visiting insects. In a couple of months or so, the gorse on the more exposed edges of the wood will start to flower, bringing splashes of golden-yellow long before the primroses dare to produce more than the odd bud.

Nettles, patches of which line most woodland paths, are opportunists, exploiting the open ground and sunlight made by the clearance of woodland. Once they were cultivated: despite their sting and their bad reputation among the more old-fashioned and over-tidy gardeners, they are useful plants in many ways. Their young leaves are edible, of course, if you are not too fussy, and they provide food for the larvae of a number of our most beautiful butterflies. You can also make a green dye from them, and the stems yield a coarse fibre that used to be made into a cloth suitable for sacks or sails. For the historians of woodland their presence, or that of their identifiable remains, is a sign of clearance, and often of felling, by humans.

It is easier to see the St John's-wort than the violets: it stands taller, beside the hawkweeds, or sow-thistles, whose most common representative, *Hieracium perpropinquum*, prefers to flower late. The hawkweeds form another group of plants which are difficult to classify unless you are a skilled botanist. There are more than 400

28

Peacock butterfly on nettle

species in Britain differing from one another in only small details.

The flowers of autumn are few and subdued, after the garishness of summer. It is less to them that you look for colour and interest now than to the fungi – not those which cohabit with the lichenicolous algae, and coat stones and bark and hang from trees, but those which fruit spectacularly on the ground. Their time is brief, but for a few weeks they have the woodland floor and they take full advantage of it. People used to think of fungi as plants; in a natural world divided simply between plants and animals, there was no other category in which to put them. But they are not really plants; they cannot use simple inorganic chemical compounds to manufacture the complex organic compounds from which all living tissues are made, and all plants can do that. Fungi feed more like animals, on food that is ready-made. So now they are placed in a kingdom of their own, the Mycota, beside the plants (Metaphyta), animals (Metazoa), and single-celled organisms which form one kingdom or two, depending on the system of classification. Most fungi produce minute fruiting-bodies – the visible parts of the fungus. Those which are large and often colourful, so that we notice them readily, belong to two major divisions: the ascomycetes, which include truffles, morels and many moulds, and the basidiomycetes which include the mushrooms and toadstools, puffballs, stinkhorns, boletes and earth stars, not to mention a number of plant parasites.

Most of us are frightened of what fungi will do to us if they have the chance. Nearly all of the mushrooms we buy, and these are the only fungi most of us in this country eat, come from farms which grow only one species, the cultivated mushroom; it is probably descended from *Agaricus brunnescens*. You will not find these in the wood in autumn; they grow in gardens and on manure-heaps, and produce their fruiting-bodies, which are the parts we eat, in summer. If you live in the country the autumn may bring small boys to the door selling field mushrooms (*Agaricus campestris*), which are close relatives of the cultivated mushroom. Though a fungus coward, I trust them because I believe the boys themselves to be the latest in a long line of part-time mushroom-pickers whose very existence testifies to their ability to pick mushrooms, not toadstools! Mushroom-pickers are subject to natural selection, like anyone else. Personally, I admire the fungi in the autumn woodlands, noting their beauty, their curious shapes, their quaint lifestyle – and leave them strictly alone. Yet some are said to be delicious to eat. I might risk a puffball, since they cannot possibly be mistaken for anything else, and all British puffballs are edible; but so far I have not found one early enough. They must be eaten while they are firm, and they change all too rapidly into a ball of fine spores which burst forth in a cloud if you touch them. I might be persuaded to try a chanterelle, which my field guide claims has the fragrance of apricots; but then a chanterelle that is just a shade darker in colour than the picture in my book could be a false chanterelle, and wreak havoc with my digestive system.

Then again, take Caesar's mushroom, *Amanita caesarea*, which the Romans are said to have eaten with relish. It is, says the book, quite unmistakable with its pretty orange cap with bits of white volva clinging to it; but I fear I might pick a few *Amanita muscaria* instead, because they look much the same to me. Fly agaric, for that is the common name of the beautiful bright red, white-flecked, hallucinogenic toadstool on which garden gnomes sit, might make me see things in a new light, but I am happy for the inside of my head to remain as it is. So I must forego the pleasures of emperors.

The 'fruiting-body', that we see and by which we identify the fungus, is no more than the reproductive organ, which produces and then releases the spores. That is why it appears only briefly. The fungus itself is there all year round. Its main part is the mycelium, a fine network of filaments which lies hidden in the soil, among dead leaves, or in the bark of a tree. It is the mycelium which obtains nutrients, and not surprisingly fungi have preferences. You will find fly agaric most commonly near birch trees, for example.

Autumn fungi are lovely to look at, but delightful to know only if you are certain you can tell one from another. The best field guide is probably *Mushrooms and Toadstools* by Geoffrey Kibby, published by Oxford University Press; but never stake your life on a picture in any book, especially with fungi, which can look quite different from their pictures. Some of the common names are very descriptive. 'Death cap' and 'panther cap' tell their own tale, and what about 'destroying angel', 'devil's bolete', or the 'poison pie' which could be mistaken for a field mushroom? With most of our fungi, no one knows whether they are poisonous or not; many are harmless, but not good to eat, some are said to be delicious. Not many of them are certainly poisonous, but among those that are, some are very deadly. So I admire them all, from a safe distance.

Most of the insects have gone by autumn, and the remaining spiders' webs catch little now. The webs themselves are deteriorating, for many spiders have died, and most of the remainder are close to doing so. Like the insects, most of our spiders spend the winter as eggs waiting to hatch. The death of one generation is part of the preparation for the next. Our most common 'garden' snail hibernates, however, and it seeks companions at this time of year, preferring to spend its winter in company, in small crevices.

Crevices are always worth examining, and especially large crevices in old trees. You may find snails there, or a wild beehive, but you may also find the remains of nests left by last summer's birds, or food debris left by an owl; you might even find bats, hanging patiently like dried leaves until it is time to emerge, flittermice that await the insects they devour in vast quantities.

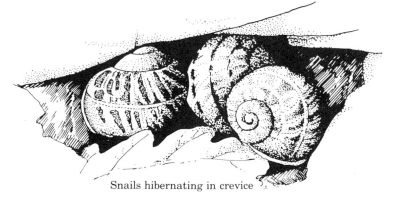

Snails hibernating in crevice

The harsh climate, thin soils and granite boulders of Dartmoor provide an improbable setting for woodland, and the woodland itself is improbable. This is Wistman's Wood. The trees are oak, they grow among the boulders, and they are contorted into fantastic shapes, yet this is no fleeting appearance of a few young trees that will soon vanish. Some of them are 400 years old (*M. Nimmo/Frank Lane Agency*)

The autumn, the time of preparation, will give way to the time for resting. Then, in winter, the trees stand out most clearly. Already the fallen leaves are turning into a kind of homogenous mush that will solidify as it freezes, and then be buried beneath the snow. The winter is scenically splendid, but apart from the resident birds which scratch a living as best they may, most of the living plants and animals, even the fungi, have paused. You may catch a glimpse of a small rodent foraging after being stirred from its nest by a sudden pang of hunger, or of a larger rodent, a squirrel perhaps. Rabbits surface now and then, but seldom move far from their burrow entrances until new grass grows green and sweet. By then the wood will be riotous with activity, and difficult to observe. You will need to stand, look, listen, and absorb quite general sensations, for should you wish to observe closely your field of view will have to be narrow. Watch a single tree, a small strip beside the path, an area no more than a few yards square if you wish to see what is really happening, but watch it closely, and visit it often. It will be almost impossible to watch the wood as a whole in spring or summer. Small though it may be, there will be far too much of it.

In winter the wood is remarkable mainly for its scenery. In spring and summer it brings sensations, evokes memories, offers welcome shade from a fierce sun, but its life is too tumultuous to be studied except on the smallest scale. In autumn, though, when the air threatens ice, the leaves are falling, and it is the colours which are riotous, you can see the wood as a whole, and at work. It becomes a unit then, a coherent system, a diverse community of organisms united in their preparation for the coming year. In autumn the inhabitants of the wood do their housework, clear away the accumulated rubbish, strip down their habitat, and so reveal it and their management of it. It is a good time to visit.

As season gives way to season in the endless round of years, the wood acquires an air of permanence. Trees live for longer than humans, woods live longer than trees, and it is tempting to suppose that our countryside that once was much more wooded had been so since the dawn of time. Because in recent years we have cleared so much woodland, and so visibly, we may persuade ourselves that the heritage we alter is much more ancient than in fact it is. Indeed, at one time Britain was almost wholly forested, but that time ended longer ago, and began more recently, than we may imagine. It is time to reflect on the history of our woodlands, and on the Atlantic Forest.

3
Atlantic Forest

The British are one of the most highly urbanised peoples in the world. Nearly four-fifths of us live in urban areas, and as our main conurbations spread and join to form what seems like one great city, at one end called Leeds and at the other London, with smaller 'megalopolises' on Tyneside and linking Glasgow and Edinburgh, it is easy to suppose that most of the country lies buried beneath buildings and roads.

The appearance is misleading. The urban areas that contain most of our population occupy less than 10 per cent of the total land area. We, the people, may be urbanised, but the land is not. Almost all of it is rural in these islands. If you look at a map and notice not the towns and cities, but the areas around them, you appreciate the size of the countryside.

It is in our towns that we expect change. Old buildings, entire blocks of old buildings, are razed, and new buildings replace them. Roads are closed to traffic, or widened, new roads are made, shops open and close again; the dynamism of city life is ceaseless, and evident everywhere. We like to think of the countryside as eternal and unchanging, and that is the way it may appear. There are people who worry about changing landscapes, but most of us see those landscapes only occasionally, and the changes may pass unremarked. The countryside of hills and valleys and rivers, of grass and flowers, hedges and trees, endures. It is there when we seek it, as it has always been. Perhaps, if we are observant of an area we know well, or if we have been warned, we notice that some hedges we saw last year are gone, or that a small wood in which we liked to walk has been cleared. Even then, the changes seem trivial.

Changes in the appearance of the countryside become apparent only when we survey a large area, over a long period of time. This provides a broader view, and our impression alters abruptly. The unchanging, timeless landscape is seen then as an artefact, a thing made largely by ourselves and our ancestors, that has changed dramatically during the few thousands of years of its human occupation. If our perspective is correct, we see that far from being eternal, our countryside is very new. It is not merely that the results of recent changes are new, but the countryside itself, the very fact of the countryside, is new when measured against the age of the rocks that lie beneath it. Humans altered the countryside they found when first they arrived, but that countryside itself had not existed for long.

Our planet is about 4,600 million years old. Its crust, on whose surface we live, is a thin layer of cool, solidified rock that sits like the skin on a cup of hot milk above a much deeper layer of hot, dense but plastic rock, the magma that now and then bursts forth to erupt from volcanoes. The crust is believed to be broken into 'tectonic' plates which move in relation to one another, carrying with them the continents that project above the surface of the oceans.

Carried on its plate, Britain has drifted about the world, and of course the climates of the world have changed. As recently as 50 million years ago, Britain enjoyed a tropical climate, and tropical evergreen forest grew where London stands today. The plants in those forests left a fossil record from which they can be identified, and many of them were close relatives of plants that grow today in tropical Asia, Australasia, Africa and America. They included palms, magnolias and other species that no longer grow naturally in Europe, although some of them have been reintroduced for ornament. Yet even then the climate was growing cooler. The tropical plants died away and were replaced, little by little, by spruce, pine, hornbeam, firs, hemlocks and other plants more familiar to us, although for many years they shared the land with such tropical survivors as certain palms and lianes. By about 2 million years ago, most of the plants in Britain were similar to those which grow here naturally today.

It was then that the climate entered a series of cycles of warmer and cooler episodes that continues to the present day. At its coldest, much of the land was sealed beneath glaciers, although they never advanced south of the Thames, and appear never to have covered the southernmost tip of Ireland. Beneath the ice, all plant life was destroyed. The soil itself was scoured away, so that when the glaciers retreated, life began again on bare gravel, sand and silt washed down with the meltwaters. Because so much water was frozen to form the ice sheets, the sea level fell and Britain was joined to continental Europe by land that now lies beneath the English Channel. At times, most of what is now the North Sea was dry land.

The weight of the ice depressed the northern part of the country, so that the newly exposed land was to be found mainly in the south.

The level of the land is still changing. The geological concept called 'isostasy', which means literally 'equal standing', holds that above a certain level in the earth, called the 'level of compensation', any column of material up to the surface will have the same mass as any other column, provided both have the same cross-sectional area. If one column is shorter than another, because at that point the crust is thinner, then it will be made from denser rock. When ice forms thickly on the surface, the underlying rocks cannot be compressed, but they are depressed and the isostatic balance is disturbed. When the ice melts, the rocks rise, and equilibrium is restored. Scandinavia and northern Scotland are rising for this reason, and the south-east of England is sinking.

Severe though the glaciations were, plants and animals were not driven from Britain altogether. In the south, beyond the edge of the ice, there was tundra growing on permafrost, and even within the ice sheets high mountains projected above the ice, exposing rock and just a little soil on which the hardiest of plants could grow. The periods of glaciation were separated. During the interglacial episodes, temperatures rose and life returned abundantly. Each glaciation and each interglacial has a name.

The story of the forests of modern Britain began during the Ipswichian interglacial, which reached its peak about 100,000 years ago, with average temperatures two or three degrees Celsius higher than they are now. It began much earlier, and birch and pine colonised a landscape formed mainly by the floodplains of great river systems. As temperatures rose further, elm and oak arrived, then hazel, which became very common. Alder and field maple, then hornbeam, arrived; for a time hornbeam was the commonest of all British trees. By the end of the period, some 50,000 to 70,000 years ago, the dominance of birch and pine indicated the cooling that heralded the return of the ice. At its warmest, however, the water chestnut (*Trapa natans*) grew in many lakes, the Montpellier maple (*Acer monspessulanum*), that today grows in southern Europe and North Africa, grew on dry land, as did verbena and *Pyracantha*. Elephant and rhinoceros were among the larger mammals.

Temperatures fell, but the ice did not return at once. For a long period the countryside was open, affording ample pasture for reindeer, bison and mammoth. With acid bogs, and woodland dominated by spruce, birch and pine, Britain at the time the next glaciation threatened must have resembled the northern Finland of today.

Then some 70,000 years ago the Devensian glaciation, to which this relatively benign period was but a prelude, buried all of Scotland, England south to about where Manchester is now, and all but the southern part of Wales and Ireland beneath the ice. It was our most recent ice age. Even beyond the limits of the ice sheet, conditions were too cold for any woodland to survive, though the reindeer, bison and mammoth did, keeping company with the lemmings. In summer, temperatures rose as high as 12 to 16°C, but in winter they hovered around −15°C, and the average temperature over a whole year was below zero. There were shrubs typical of tundra, such as willows and juniper, but the open countryside was dominated by flowering herbs. Where shallow pools formed over the permafrost, under conditions of high evaporation, salt-tolerant species of shrubs and herbs thrived in habitats very similar to those found today in parts of eastern Greenland and Siberia.

Such Arctic pools provide a harsh environment. The water that flows in to fill them carries with it mineral salts dissolved from the soil and rocks. Bright sunshine and dry winds evaporate water from the surface of the pools, so they need no outlet. Water leaves only by evaporation. What evaporates is pure water, leaving behind the salts, just as common salt (sodium chloride) can be made by evaporating brine, and the pools become more and more saline. The water may be clear – but that is because most plants and animals find it deadly.

Within any glaciation there are interstadials, warmer periods during which the glaciers retreat partially. But still the soils remain too poor, the winds too fierce, for the establishment of woodland. Indeed, botanists define an 'interstadial' as a period of generally warmer conditions that are still too cool, or last too short a time, to permit temperate deciduous forest to develop in areas where it would grow during a full interglacial.

Humans had lived in Britain intermittently since long before the start of the Ipswichian. Generally they seem to have preferred interstadials to full interglacials; when they settled during an interglacial they did so at its beginning or end, when conditions were cooler. They lived by hunting large game, and their preference for cooler conditions and for the habitat close to the edges of the ice was not mere perversity. We may think of this tundra as barren and incapable of supporting much life, but although it is harsh, in its own way it is rich. The soil scoured away by the ice is washed down by meltwater to form thick fertile beds. During the summer plant growth is rapid, and though winters are hard, the open landscape provides sufficient food for large herds of herbivorous animals. The humans thrived in the tundra because that is where their prey thrived. During full interglacials, when the countryside became forested, opportunities for large grazing animals were reduced, and the humans retreated.

There were at least four major interstadials during the Devensian, and humans took advantage of all of them. In the earlier periods most probably it was Neanderthal people (*Homo sapiens neanderthalensis*) who settled. Later it was modern humans (*Homo sapiens sapiens*), people exactly like ourselves. It was only during the coldest periods, when the ice extent was at its maximum, that humans seem to have been absent. We may picture an 'ice age' as a long period during which vast areas lie beneath ice sheets, but even when the interstadials are excluded, conditions are at their most extreme for only part of the time. Although the Devensian lasted for 40,000 to 60,000 years, Britain was ice-covered for no more than 3,000 years in the south and 15,000 years in the north. It was quite a possible place to live in.

By about 20,000 years ago the climate was growing warmer again, the ice retreating. This warming led to the last interstadial, called the Allerød after the site in Denmark whose fossil pollen record provided the first clear evidence of it. It lasted from about 18,000 to about 12,000 years ago. It was followed by a brief return to colder conditions, but the Devensian glaciation had come to an end, and by about 10,000 years ago Britain was entering a new interglacial, called the Flandrian. That interglacial has continued to the present day. We are living in an interglacial and most scientists agree that one day the ice will return.

The Allerød was sandwiched between two cooler periods, both of them marked by the presence of mountain avens (*Dryas octopetala*), a low creeping shrub typical of Arctic or Alpine conditions, and for this reason known as the Older and Younger *Dryas*. The temporary return of colder climatic conditions during the Younger *Dryas* may have reduced the wooded area greatly, and the forests may have disappeared.

During the Allerød, however, grasses, sedges, and willows colonised large areas. They were followed by downy birch (*Betula pubescens*) and silver birch (*B. pendula*), the silver birch being less widespread and confined mainly to the south. The dwarf birch (*B. nana*) and Arctic willow (*Salix herbacea*), which are more typical of tundra and are intolerant of warmth, became less common. Gradually the countryside changed, became less open, with copses and in some places extensive forests forming. Aspen (*Populus tremula*) arrived, and rowan (*Sorbus aucuparia*), and the birch

39

Mountain avens

forests included much Scots pine (*Pinus sylvestris*). Replacement of the more Arctic vegetation was not complete: species which retreated did not disappear entirely.

From late Devensian times, no change in the British flora has been complete. Always there are relics, small corners in which older communities continue to find the conditions which suit them. Today you may find plants typical of the final millennia of the last glaciation growing on mountains, wherever the soil accumulates in sufficient quantity to support them. Dwarf birch, a tundra plant, continues to grow in parts of Scotland and in Teesdale. Juniper can still be found growing on chalk and limestone soils in the south of England, and on a wider range of soils in the uplands of Wales and Scotland. The rise and decline of the juniper is especially important as an indicator of climatic change. It can survive as a small shrub in the tundra. When temperatures rise it responds by growing larger and producing seeds, so that its increase indicates a climatic improvement. As the higher temperatures are sustained, and larger trees begin to colonise, the juniper is shaded and becomes less common.

By about 10,000 years ago the new interglacial had begun, and the juniper was declining. The countryside then was heathlike, with grasses, sedges, crowberry, juniper and willow, and flowering herbs such as meadowsweet (*Filipendula ulmaria*). They gave way, probably rapidly, to birch forest. The seeds of birch are light and easily dispersed over long distances by the wind: the birch woods became dense, but it was not long before they were invaded by Scots pine and aspen. Then, and for many years to come, Britain remained linked to continental Europe across what is now the Channel, and the rather park-like vegetation was continuous. The sea around Britain was at least 100 feet lower than it is now, possibly 300 feet lower; the figures are not known precisely. Large parts of the Irish and North Seas were dry land.

As the climate continued to grow warmer, the most sheltered areas were colonised by species that could not have tolerated the temperatures of the late glacial period. The strawberry tree (*Arbutus unedo*) entered western Ireland, for example, and formed part of a vegetation pattern more typical today of the Mediterranean region. That pattern still survives locally in parts of southwest Ireland, where there are *Arbutus* woods, and in southern Cornwall.

More generally the birch was joined by hazel and pine. Then, by about 8,000 years ago, elm (*Ulmus*, almost certainly *U. glabra*, the wych-elm) and oak (*Quercus*, but it is impossible to tell which species) arrived, two genera that require much warmer conditions. Clearly the climate was becoming temperate. By 7,500 years ago holly (*Ilex aquifolium*), which had arrived rather earlier, was establishing itself as far north as central Scotland. It is another indicator of climatic change and, as we shall see later, of human activity. It can grow to timber size, and in the past has done so; entire woods dominated by holly used to be common. Yet it is intolerant of cold and drought. It can survive in a mildly continental climate, such as that of eastern Britain today, but it really thrives only in an oceanic climate. Its spread suggests strongly that the British climate was becoming more oceanic, more like the climate we have today.

By about 7,500 years ago the ice had melted sufficiently for the seas to have returned to their interglacial levels. Britain became an island and the warmer conditions, revealed by the examination of pollen from soils that can be dated, mark the beginning of the Atlantic Period, which lasted for 2,500 years.

Small-leaved lime, or winter linden (*Tilia cordata*), demands warm conditions. It has been here for nearly 10,000 years, but from about 7,500 years ago it was becoming more abundant; it is another indicator of climatic improvement. Humans used the foliage of this lime for fodder for their livestock, its wood for timber, and its bark for fibre. This is believed to have led to its over-exploitation and decline although a later deterioration in the climate may have contributed. The large-leaved lime (*T. platyphyllos*) was much less common, although it was growing here 7,500 years ago.

Dates, and the division of time into periods on the basis of the pollen record of the plants that grew, can be misleading. One period does not end and another begin precisely: they shade into one another, and the reading of past climates from a reconstruction of vegetation patterns is a matter of emphasis. After all, the climate is not constant from one year to another, or from one place or another, and a species which requires particular conditions may find them on an exposed hillside, or in a sheltered valley, while the climate prevailing over the country as a whole, taken as an average over centuries, is unfavourable. The plants recorded as being here are those whose pollen has been found and identified. No doubt others were here, too, whose remains have not been discovered. The dates, then, and the estimates of the composition of plant communities, are useful as a guide, and should not be taken as final, definitive statements.

Little by little Britain was becoming forested, as was most of western Europe. In time the forest extended over most of the continent and was so vast and so unified that it is called simply the Atlantic Forest, after the climatic period in which it occurred. It did not reach the mountain peaks, of course, or to high ground within reach of the salt-laden winds off the Atlantic Ocean, but wherever trees could grow, they grew. The British part of the Atlantic Forest is often called the 'wildwood'; it is the ecological pattern we take to be the most 'natural' in these islands under the climatic conditions of the Atlantic Period.

The term 'wildwood', coined by Dr Oliver Rackham, refers to the original primeval woodland that the first humans found when they arrived in Britain; so it is useful, despite its fanciful *Wind in the Willows* associations. There is some confusion about the terms 'forest', 'wood' and 'woodland', each having a precise meaning for some people, but being used interchangeably by others. In this book, therefore, the original forest will be called the wildwood, and use of any of the other terms is deliberate.

The wildwood is 'natural' because it is the final, climax stage of the succession that followed the changes in climate during the earlier millennia of our present interglacial, the Flandrian. Many of the colonising species crossed into Britain by land, but by the time the wildwood was fully established sea levels had risen, and Great

Britain (present-day England, Wales and Scotland) was an island, isolated from continental Europe and from Ireland. Essentially the process was complete.

Ash (*Fraxinus excelsior*) was here, albeit sparsely, around 9,000 years ago; by 7,500 years ago it was fairly common in north-west England and by 2,000 years ago it was widespread, but still mainly in the north. Field maple (*Acer campestre*) was here by 4,000 years ago; beech (*Fagus sylvatica*) was present 8,000 years ago and was widespread, mainly in southern England, by 4,000 years ago; hornbeam (*Carpinus betulus*) was also present here some 8,000 years ago and fairly widespread by 4,000 years ago.

The status of beech used to be questioned, because in his description of south-eastern England Julius Caesar suggested it was absent from areas where it is now common. It is likely, though, that he used the name *fagus* to describe the sweet chestnut, which we know was introduced, for it seems certain that our beech was well established by his time. Several of the tree species that flourished in Great Britain did not reach Ireland, probably because the rising sea level was an insuperable barrier to them: field maple and hornbeam are examples.

It is widely accepted by ecologists that this ancient wildwood contained the only species of trees that are truly native to Britain. Other species, attractive and valuable though they may be, are immigrants or, more botanically, 'exotics'. At first glance the distinction may seem arbitrary. The historical record, over very recent geological time, shows that the flora of Britain, or for that matter of any other part of our planet, changes constantly and, provided the time-scale used is long enough, changes extensively. The word 'native' should be used with caution when applied to plants. *Rhododendron ponticum*, for example, is a large shrub which is 'native' to the countries surrounding the Black Sea; it has been introduced to Britain and flourishes here, to the delight of some people and the distress of others. It did not grow in Britain during the earlier stages of the Flandrian, but it was widespread in Ireland in a much earlier interglacial, the Hoxnian. Can a plant cease to be a 'native' when it leaves, becoming an 'immigrant' when it returns later? Ecologically, yes it can, and although apparently arbitrary the distinction between 'native' and 'exotic' species is useful. The Woodland Trust, for example, strongly encourages the planting of native species in preference to all others.

There are several reasons. Plant species which were carried here as seeds by wind, birds or the feet of animals moving across land that now lies beneath the Channel, took their chances. If they

43

survived it was because they fell in places where their needs were supplied. They had no special protection. As they bred and their descendants colonised new areas they had to accommodate themselves to the conditions and communities they found, so over the generations entire communities of plants, and the animals feeding on the plants, developed together. By and large, therefore, native tree species 'fit in' better. There are more animals adapted to the foods and shelter they provide. As they take nutrients from the soil and as their leaves fall, local soil populations of micro-organisms, fungi and animals are more likely to be able to live with them. Thus they are able to contribute to the communities in which they find themselves.

Species that were introduced later, by humans, often were brought here to satisfy human requirements for food, timber or other products, or simply for decoration. They may well grow successfully, sometimes prolifically, but the communities into which they are planted have more difficulty adapting to their presence. Sometimes they may have great difficulty. The rhododendron that was present in the distant past and has been introduced in modern times has adapted itself to British conditions, but in some places at the expense of the older vegetation, so it invades and replaces not merely other trees and shrubs, but many of the smaller plants and animals associated with them. Sycamore has had a similar effect in many places.

The early species, then, are 'natives'. It may be, of course, that as humans crossed into Britain they brought plants with them. Seeds would have lodged in their clothes and in the goods they carried with them, and some of those seeds would have germinated. We cannot know, but it is not important because the distinction lies between plants that arrived fortuitously and those that were brought here deliberately to be planted and tended. This does not mean, however, that the humans living here as the ice sheets retreated were passive, and played no part in shaping their environment. They were environmental manipulators, like all species, as we shall see.

The wildwood was not uniform in its composition, and the changes that had caused it to grow continued, so change itself continued. Around lakes and on wet ground, but rarely in the far west or in the Scottish highlands, there were woods of alder. In lowland England, as far north as modern Lancashire, lime forests developed. On high ground the vegetation was more often dominated by birch or pine. Elm and hazel woods were common almost everywhere, and oak-hazel woods were most common on high ground. In what is now northern England, ash often grew alongside oak instead of hazel. The 'traditional' picture of the mighty oak woodlands of England is largely false: the wildwood contained oak, certainly, but it was much more diverse, more dynamic, than that old view suggests.

Lime was much commoner than oak at first, then began to disappear. It does not set seed in our climate, reproducing vegetatively, and early farmers cleared away much of it. They had many uses for it, and they wanted to cultivate the soils on which it grew. Perhaps because they occur on heavier land that was unworkable to the first farmers, far fewer oak stands were cleared, so in time oak became relatively more common.

Lime was declining from about 5,000 years ago, and elm was declining at much the same time, its place being taken mainly by ash. It too seems to have suffered at the hands of early farmers, who may have cropped its foliage to feed their livestock, which were kept in stalls, probably as a defence against predators. There are farmers who keep their animals in this way even today in parts of eastern Europe and western Asia.

The humans who came to live in Britain during the Devensian, and who stayed as the wildwood expanded its area, did not live in isolation from the vegetation around them. They did not merely hunt game without disturbing the trees, as used to be supposed: from the very start they manipulated their environment, probably using fire to drive game as well as to clear the land, and almost certainly encouraging the plants they found most useful. The trees and the humans were partners who became rivals in a competition the humans were bound to win, and eventually the wildwood was tamed.

That taming, as a result of which the management of woodland attained high levels of sophistication, is considered in a later chapter.

4
Woods and Trees

The British portion of the ancient Atlantic Forest, the original wildwood, was much more diverse than tradition may suggest. Far from being a solid mass of more or less impenetrable vegetation, dominated by oak and perhaps two or three other tree species, it varied widely from place to place. In some places it was absent, and the landscape was open and treeless, or heathy – open country with isolated trees. In others the tree canopy was open, so it was easy to move among the trees, and enough sunlight reached the ground for grasses and other herbs that are intolerant of shade to grow. Even where the canopy was closed, the composition of the wildwood differed from one place to another. We need, therefore, to delve more deeply into the history of the trees that formed the wildwood, and also some of those which have been introduced more recently but are now important woodland species; and we must also look at the types of woodland in which they occur.

The convention by which certain species are considered 'native' and others not was mentioned in the previous chapter. This is relevant to any consideration of the history of British woodlands, and to today's efforts to conserve or replace by new planting what is most ecologically important. But when we examine modern woodlands we must take account of species that have been introduced. No matter how it arrives in Britain, either a species will grow in our woodlands without human assistance or it will not. Those that were introduced by humans, but which have become established and now spread by their own means are said to be 'naturalised'. Others acclimatise with more difficulty and may never establish themselves outside plantations where they have some protection from the hazards of life in the unmanaged countryside. Some of these are important nevertheless, for they have been planted for ornament, to enhance landscapes.

The word 'forest' is itself the source of some confusion. These days we use it to describe an area of land covered with trees, often trees that have been planted by humans we call 'foresters'. The verb 'to forest' means to plant with trees. This is not the original meaning of the word, however, and the older meaning survives, especially in place names: 'forest' comes from the Latin word *foris*, 'outside'. Originally, the forest was the land which lay beyond the cultivated and enclosed farm land. The forest was unfenced; it might or might not be covered with trees. In the uplands it was often quite open, but it was no less 'forest' for that. In Norman times some of this unfenced land which was not being used was reserved for hunting, mainly of deer; much of it was held for the use of the sovereign. Its use was regulated by a body of law. So 'forest' tended to be the term used for an area of land whose use was subject to 'forest law'. Much of the forest which was once tree-covered has since been cleared, but the word 'forest' may be retained in the name – as in Dartmoor Forest or Sherwood Forest for example. So 'forest' has three meanings: unenclosed land lying beyond the limits of the farm land; land at one time reserved for hunting and protected by forest law; and land on which trees are grown. 'Woodland' is much less ambiguous, although it suggests a smaller area than a 'forest'.

Looking at the types of woodland that occur in Britain, we have to remember that all woodland changes. It has changed in the past and it is changing now, in many small, subtle ways that in time may lead to more radical change. This is not the gross change wrought by humans, but the change that results from the interactions of plants and non-human animals.

At one time people believed that evolution proceeds as species adapt to a chemical and physical environment over which they have no control. We know now that the process is more complex, and much more interesting.

There is and can be no sharp distinction between the living and non-living components of an environment, for the non-living components are under the firm control of the living, which manipulate them constantly. This manipulation operates on a global scale, to maintain conditions on the planet that are congenial to living organisms, but it also operates on a local scale. It can be seen wherever a new habitat is colonised by a succession of plants, each of which must find space and nutrient for itself. In finding that space and nutrient, each plant alters its own immediate surroundings, and each new arrival has to regard the earlier arrivals as part of the 'given' environment in which it must satisfy its needs. Human management may distort the process, or arrest it, and that too is a manipulation of the environment.

As trees grow, shading out many herbs and shrubs, they transpire into the air water drawn from the soil, and deposit organic matter on the surface. This may affect the movement of water through the soil, and increase – or more probably decrease – the amount of water available to other plants. The acidity of the soil may change as leaves and decaying wood are converted to humus. The selection of particular mineral nutrients taken by one species may alter the balance of nutrients remaining in the soil, so favouring certain other species which prefer the new balance, and discouraging species which flourished under the former conditions. Even a climax community, in which all space is occupied, and all the necessary ingredients for plant life are in use, may change if changes in the world outside impinge on it.

In the following section I have listed the species of trees in alphabetical order of their most familiar English names, adding the botanical name for the sake of clarity since some have more than one common name. Not all the species listed dominate woodland in which they occur and give their names to it, but the role of each species in woodland is contained within the description of the species itself.

Because there are many types of woodland it is necessary to have some system for naming them. Conventionally they are named after the tree species that seems most characteristic: usually it is the species that grows tallest, or exerts the strongest influence on the community and its environment. The convention can seem misleading, however. The species which gives its name to a woodland is very unlikely to be the only species present there, and it may not be even the species that is most immediately conspicuous. It is not impossible to visit a wood and have some trouble finding the species after which the wood is named! If you should experience this, remember that the most influential tree may not be the most obvious one, or that the wood may have changed since the last time it was surveyed, or that its association with a particular tree species may be traditional even though the species itself is now uncommon.

Because a plant community is usually so complex, defining it is more difficult than it may seem and over the years many ecologists have devised systems for dealing with the problem. A. G. Tansley was probably the first, back in the 1930s, and since then O. Rackham and G. F. Peterken have refined the task. There is not room here to discuss in detail what amounts to a highly mathematical concept, but I can outline the broad approach and the reasons for it. Suppose you visited a wood and wished to discuss it later with someone who had never seen it. You would need some general way to describe its type and probably you would want to use the names of the most common trees. How would you discover which trees were most abundant? You might try laying down a straight line right through the wood, walking along it, and making a note of each tree species you met. Then you could add up the numbers for each species. But what if your line crossed a stream with wet ground beside it? Different trees, alder or willow perhaps, would grow there. Does this make it a different kind of wood? There is no simple answer.

Perhaps you should abandon the use of dominant species altogether. After all, it can be argued that species which are common are so because they can tolerate a wide range of environmental conditions. It might be better, therefore, to use species which have very particular requirements and so are likely to be characteristic of the environments in which they occur. This sounds like a good idea. The trouble is that such species are uncommon, even rare, and in your study of an area you might not find a single individual.

Traditionally, British woods have been described by the species which dominate them. In Europe and North America ecologists place more emphasis on groups of species rather than just one or two dominants, and consider those groups as social units. This forms the basis for phytosociology, essentially the study of plant communities.

All this is mentioned only to demonstrate that what may appear simple and straightforward is not simple at all.

While on the subject of classification I should say something about the way species are named scientifically.

The system was first devised by the Swedish botanist Carl von Linné (1707–78), who is better known by his own Latin name, Linnaeus. His problem was that then, as now, common names for plants or animals vary from place to place – even within a single country and language – and the same common name may apply to more than one kind of organism. It is difficult for people from different places to hold intelligent conversations without finding themselves at cross purposes. So Linnaeus arranged all organisms in hierarchical groups. First those which are generally similar are grouped together, and the group is given a generic name; then a specific name is given to each member of the group. Thus each species has two names – in Latin, an international tradition. The first name, with a capital letter, is that of the genus, or group; the second is that of the species. For example, a group of trees that all share certain important characteristics is given a name, say *Quercus*. Any particular species within that group is given a name of its own, say *robur*. The hierarchy can then be extended upward and downward. You can group together genera to make families: *Quercus* is placed in the family Fagaceae, which also includes the beeches. Groups of families form orders, groups of orders form classes, groups of classes form divisions (or phyla in the case of animals), and groups of divisions form kingdoms. At lower levels the species may be divided into subspecies or, in plants, varieties.

The science of naming organisms in this way is called taxonomy; each group at any level is a taxon (plural taxa) and the person who does the naming is a taxonomist. For plants, the allocation and registration of names is governed by the International Code of Botanical Nomenclature and the rules are strict.

That, you might think, should be that, but it is not because in solving one question it raises another. What are those important characteristics that define each of the groups above the level of species? The definition of a species is not too difficult, because it comprises a group of organisms that reproduce among themselves to produce new individuals closely resembling their parents, but cannot produce fertile offspring by breeding with members of any other group. At levels above that of the species, definition becomes more difficult: it must be based on as many characteristics as possible, but the characteristics must be weighted so that some are regarded as more important than others. These days the characteristics relate to the ancestry of the species and, increasingly, its genetic composition.

Nevertheless, different taxonomists use different methods, and from time to time names change. It is usual, therefore, to include in any formal classification the name, or abbreviation of the name (as Linn., or L., for Linnaeus), of the original taxonomist, cited as an authority. There are many taxonomists; the abbreviations of their personal names used below are standardised. Where more than one set of initials is included the first refers to the naming of the genus, the second to the species. (If you would like to know more about plant taxonomy I recommend the book by C. Jeffrey listed in Further Reading.)

At the end of the description of some of the species and woodland types there is a list of good examples, arranged in alphabetical order of the counties or regions in which they are situated. They are not necessarily the best woods of their type in Britain, and certainly they are not the only ones. They are included because the Woodland Trust or I have some reliable information about them. In the Directory at the end of the book more details are given about their precise location and any restrictions there may be on visiting them.

50

Alder (*Alnus glutinosa* (L.) Gaertn.)

Only one species of alder grows freely in Britain, the common or black alder, although several others are planted as ornamentals. It grew here during certain earlier Pleistocene interglacials, and it may have entered the country again during the latter years of the Devensian glaciation. It is less common in northern Scotland and the Irish Midlands than over the rest of the country.

It prefers wet sites, but not those which are inundated permanently. From time to time the soil in which it grows must dry fairly thoroughly. So you are likely to find it on land that is prone to periodic flooding, except where a clay soil forms an impermeable layer that retains water close to the surface. Otherwise it has no special preference for particular soils, is fairly indifferent to soil acidity, and because its roots possess nodules of nitrogen-fixing bacteria can thrive in relatively infertile soils, usually improving their fertility.

It is of little value as fuel or timber, although carpenters and wood-turners make some use of it because it is easy to work. It is also easy to treat with wood preservatives, and is used for estate work. In pre-medieval times it was used widely for piling and making trackways, probably because it was abundant and easy to work. Later it was the preferred tree for making charcoal. It has also been coppiced and used for making clogs.

Although it is often a small, rather scrubby tree, an alder can grow to a height of 60ft or more.

A woodland dominated by alder is called 'carr', although that term is often extended to fen woodlands and areas of scrub where it is not especially common. There are three types of true carr, found on fenland, in river valleys and on level upland plateaux. The tree colonises suitable sites readily, its seeds being transported by water, and to a lesser extent by wind.

The most extensive fenland carrs, found in the Norfolk Broads, are the result of recent colonisation of areas that formerly were meadow. In valleys, alder may line rivers and streams, sometimes in the company of crack willow, ash or blackthorn, or adjacent to stands of chestnut or hornbeam. On upland plateaux, alder is sometimes found on the watershed, growing in mixed woodland commonly dominated by lime (in East Anglia) or birch, and merging gradually into adjacent woodland containing no alder; often it is on a sandy or silty soil layer which overlies clay.

There are good examples of alder woodland in several parts of the country (see list overleaf).

Cambridgeshire: Wicken Fen.
Durham: Witton le Wear nature reserve.
Gwynedd: Coed Dolgarrog Ardda Alderwood nature reserve.
Highland Region: Mount Alderwoods National Nature Reserve.
Norfolk: Bure Marshes National Nature Reserve.
Staffordshire: Himley Wood.
Strathclyde and Central Regions: Loch Lomond mainland woods National Nature Reserve.

Ash (*Fraxinus excelsior* L.)
Ash seems to have been absent from Britain right up to the end of the Devensian glaciation, and it appeared rather late in the present interglacial. Once established, however, it spread rapidly and became very common, except in Scotland and Ireland. It is an impressive tree, growing to 130ft or more, and although only one species grows freely in Britain, there are several varieties, each with different habits; more exotic species have been introduced but do not grow in woodlands – except in the rare cases where they have been planted.

The late arrival of ash may be due to its preference for warmth, and its spread may be due to human activity. As it advanced so elm and lime declined, and it is possible that when the elm and lime were cropped to provide browse for livestock, ash profited by invading vacant sites. Ash is intolerant of shade, and so in time it tends to be replaced, usually by beech and oak which form climax communities. It may be, therefore, that ash was quite widespread in the original forest but common only locally.

An ash tree can live for 200 years or so, but if it is coppiced, cut down close to ground level so that the stump sends up many slim, straight stems, the stools can survive for much longer. At Bradfield Woods, in West Suffolk, there is an ash stool said to be about 1,000 years old and 18ft in diameter. Ash stools are often large, but if the report is correct this is the largest.

The tough, elastic wood has many uses, but it is best known as the traditional material for the handles and hafts of tools; it is also used to make hockey sticks and tennis rackets, and in coach building. Indeed, at one time it was used to make many things that these days are made from metal, and it used to be grown in hedgerows for cropping.

Of all British woodland trees, ash is the most prolific producer of seed. It reproduces in this way, unlike many trees, for its seeds can remain dormant for several years before germinating; and the seedlings, unlike the mature trees, are tolerant of shade, and will

52

wait many years until an opening in the canopy gives them the light they need to grow to full size.

Only in woodlands on very acid soil does ash form more than three-quarters of the tree population. There it is found in the company of hornbeam or lime, on ground covered with bramble, but with primroses and stinging nettle wherever sunlight penetrates, and sometimes with great carpets of bluebells. Ash is unusual in requiring a rare combination of well-drained but wet, fertile but acid, conditions. As soils become rather less acid, the ash may be associated with hazel more commonly than hornbeam, and field maple may join these species. There are exceptions, however, and ash can occur on chalk or lime where the uppermost soil horizons are sufficiently acid. There are splendid ash woods in Derbyshire, growing on a soil formed from limestone bedrock. (A cross-section cut vertically through a soil reveals distinct layering, and the layers are known scientifically as 'horizons'. Each horizon has its own characteristics and it is by their horizons that soils are classified taxonomically.)

There are good examples of ash woodland in several parts of the country.

Cambridgeshire: Aversley Wood, where ash is being managed to prevent it dominating the woodland.
Clwyd: Bigwood, which consists of mature oak and ash woodland on a limestone soil.
Devon: Axmouth National Nature Reserve.
Dyfed: Coed Tyddyn du, where ash is being managed to prevent it dominating the woodland.
Highland Region: Rassal National Nature Reserve.
North Yorkshire: Colt Park, in the Ribblehead Woods National Nature Reserve.
Powys: Penmoelallt.
Somerset: Rodney Stoke National Nature Reserve and Ebbor Gorge National Nature Reserve.

Aspen (*Populus tremula* L.)
The aspen is a tree of northern habitats, and has grown in Britain since late in the Devensian, making it one of our oldest residents. Today it occurs in ancient woodlands, especially in the east of England. It can grow on soils with a wide range of acidity, preferring rather heavy soils that are wet in spring. It reproduces vegetatively by suckering, forming clones, and sometimes these are extensive. In Stisted Wood, Essex, for example, aspens dominate

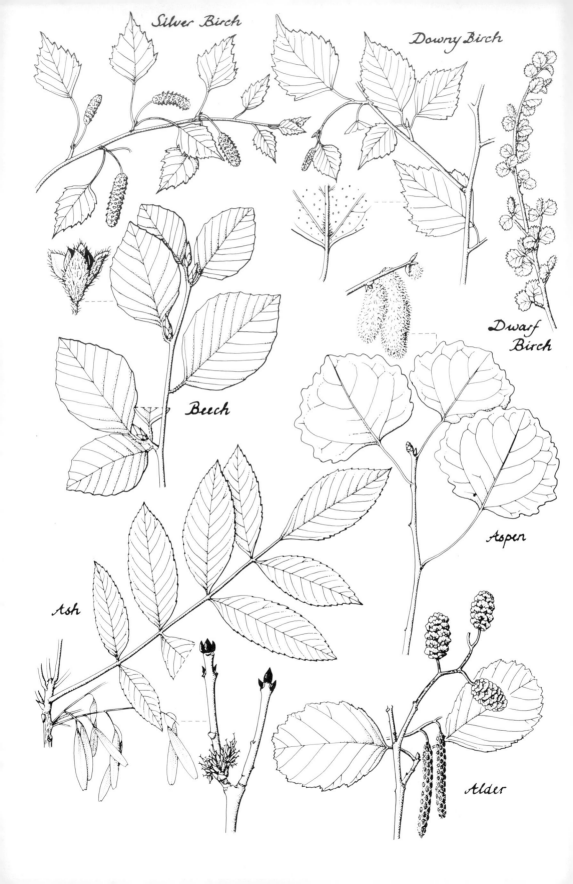

Silver Birch

Downy Birch

Dwarf Birch

Beech

Aspen

Ash

Alder

some 10 acres. The suckers are intolerant of shade, however, and the trees are short-lived. When they do reproduce by seed, the seedlings (unlike the mature trees) are highly susceptible to drought; their large water requirement demands weather conditions that are rarely met in Britain.

The tree is most common on plateaux that are wet at some time of the year, and in the company of lime, field maple, hornbeam and hazel, although it is only weakly competitive and these other species often crowd it out. Nevertheless, clones of aspen can be found in many woods.

Its leaves grow on long stalks and are covered on their undersides with fine hairs, so they move in the slightest breeze, as though trembling, and the shivering of aspen leaves makes the tree easy to identify. It also gives rise to the old legend that Jesus was crucified on a cross made from aspen wood and the tree has shivered in horror ever since.

Beech (*Fagus sylvatica* L.)
Beech also arrived late, and for a long time was uncommon. Today it is fairly widespread, but this is due to planting, and has produced some fine woodlands, in Epping Forest for example, and Enfield Chase, in Middlesex. Its expansion, after many centuries of being confined to local woodlands, may have been assisted by the clearance of the original forest; it entered as an opportunist species of secondary woodland. Its expansion did not really begin until the Iron Age. Even so, the history of the tree remains shrouded in mystery. It is fairly easy to work and to treat with wood preservatives, and it is strong. It was used in the Chilterns to make furniture, and this may explain why it was planted, but it has never been really popular for its wood, at least until modern times, although it was much used for fuel and especially for making charcoal.

Britain seems to lie at the very edge of the geographic range for beech. Probably in response to conditions it usually finds difficult, it produces seed on average only once every three years, and then does so abundantly. This stratagem makes it impossible for predators to rely on it, and although they will take full advantage of the occasional abundance many seeds are left uneaten and may germinate. Beech will not colonise open ground, growing up only beneath the shelter of bushes or other trees, but abandoned farm land that has been colonised already by other species may give way to beech wood, and beeches frequently appear in gaps between trees in other types of woodland. In some places it has replaced lime and

55

oak in what had been considered climax woodland, and so has come to dominate woods in which formerly it was a minor component. So it is possible that it has not yet reached the full extent of its range and in time beech might become the true climax species in many areas.

Beech will grow on almost any soil that is well drained, and it tolerates a wide range of acidity. Although it is sensitive to changes in climate, it is much less so to brief changes in weather, and survives well during short periods of cold. Its seedlings and saplings, however, cannot survive much frost.

Where beech woods have been planted they can be rather monotonous. Elsewhere, however, they support a variety of other species, including sweet chestnut, field maple and hazel.

There are good examples of beech woodland in several parts of the country.

Buckinghamshire: Chesham Bois Wood.
Gloucestershire: Cotswold Commons and Beechwoods National Nature Reserve, Frith Wood nature reserve, and Parish and Oldhills Woods.
Gwent: Cym Clydach National Nature Reserve.
Hampshire: Selborne Hanger.
Hertfordshire: Fox Covert and Fordhams Wood nature reserve.
Nottinghamshire: Hannah Wood.
Oxfordshire: Aston Rowant Woods National Nature Reserve.

Birch (*Betula* L. species)
Dwarf birch (*B. nana* L.), the shrub-like plant of the tundra which grew in Britain during the Devensian, is now confined almost entirely to northern Scotland. The tree birches entered by late in the Devensian, spread throughout the country, and then retreated somewhat as the climax forest became established. There are two species, *B. pendula* Roth. (silver or white birch) and *B. pubescens* Ehrh. (downy birch), and they are impossible to distinguish historically, because the remains they leave are virtually identical. In more recent times *B. pubescens* has been the commoner.

Birch produces large amounts of pollen. This, combined with the fact that it used to grow in the Fens and on the Somerset Levels, where remains were preserved, may have caused it to be over-represented in the fossil record, at least in the lowlands; it may have been less common than the record suggests.

Birch produces strong wood that is fairly easy to work and to treat with wood preservatives. It has played an important part in human history. Indeed, at one time it was so valuable that the economy of Scotland and northern England was based on its products. It was used for making barrels, especially those in which herring were stored, for wood-turning, for making furniture and for estate work, as well as being a good raw material for making charcoal. In Scotland its twigs were used to make besoms, and throughout Britain to make switches with which young people were beaten. The bark has also been used for tanning leather, especially in Russia.

Birches are short-lived, but produce multitudes of winged seeds that are dispersed by wind and germinate readily. This makes it a primary coloniser and very invasive, especially of land that has been cleared and then abandoned by humans. You may find it on industrial wasteland that has been left undisturbed for some time. It can form pure stands at a considerable distance from its parent woodland. Once established, birch tends to be persistent for a time, then giving way to other dominant species. On lowland heaths, such as those of Hampshire and Surrey, birch is often replaced by pine, which in turn gives way to oak. In other places the pine stage may be omitted. Most naturally occurring woodland contains some birch.

Although it may invade anywhere and birch woods can be found throughout Britain, especially on lowland heaths, today it is primarily a tree of the uplands. In Scotland it is the most common woodland dominant. Downy birch may form pure stands, or stands containing some silver birch; rowan may also thrive in birch woods on high ground, adjacent to open moorland above. Elsewhere, birch is most likely to be found growing in the company of chestnut, sometimes with some hornbeam and hazel.

Birch woods occur in most parts of Britain. The list below comprises only a brief selection of examples.

Grampian Region: Morrone Wood National Nature Reserve.
Highland Region: Inverpolly Woods National Nature Reserve.
Huntingdonshire: Holme Fen National Nature Reserve.
Staffordshire: Himley Wood.

Box (*Buxus sempervirens* L.)

The pollen of box has been found at one site in the Lake District, and has been dated to a time before it could have been introduced by humans. So the tree has been established as part of the prehistoric, Flandrian flora. The Romans made much use of it, but there is no reason to suppose they introduced it, since some of their products were different ones from those in southern Europe. Today there are many introduced species, but the original common box still forms small woods, in Surrey and the Cotswolds, and some places are named after it, such as Box Hill in Surrey.

Cherry (*Prunus* L. species)
The wild cherry or gean (*Prunus avium* L.) has grown in Britain at least since neolithic times. It is fairly large, up to 80ft, and grows readily and rapidly from seed or suckers. Its fruits are edible, but small, and the tree has been used mainly for timber.

P. padus L., the bird-cherry, a tree similar to the wild cherry, has grown in Britain since the start of the present interglacial, and may be found throughout the country, but mainly in northern Britain, Wales and East Anglia.

The wild cherry has a scattered distribution throughout Great Britain. Sometimes it occurs in hedges, but in East Anglia it often grows in woodland, forming clumps that grow from suckers. It can dominate woodland, alone or with a co-dominant species, and does so in one or two woods in Suffolk and Essex. In truly ancient woods it often grows near the woodland edge, and although it is not invasive it can form secondary woodland. It prefers a rather acid soil, which may assist it in colonising cleared land that is too acid for most tree species, but this does not preclude it from calcareous soils. You will find it in the Chilterns, for example.

Other *Prunus* species, such as blackthorn or sloe (*P. spinosa* L.), are more confined to hedgerows, although the bird-cherry can occur as underwood in ash and hazel woodland, where this is on calcareous soils: it replaces some of the hazel. It can extend elsewhere, most notably into lime woods and plateau alder woodland.

Chestnut
Two quite unrelated trees bear the common name 'chestnut'. The sweet or Spanish chestnut, *Castanea sativa* Mill., was brought to Britain during the Iron Age. It has been said that the Romans introduced it, but they may have imported only its timber. The presence of nuts or their remains at archaeological sites does not prove the tree was being grown, as the nuts themselves could have been imports. Certainly the tree has been planted widely, deliberately or accidentally, by people who have carried the nuts around with them, and at one time it was planted on quite a large scale for use as coppice. The tree has established itself in the wild, however, and by medieval times it was growing in ecological niches it had defined for itself. It is at its far geographical limit in Britain, but unlike some other introduced species in this position it has become fully naturalised.

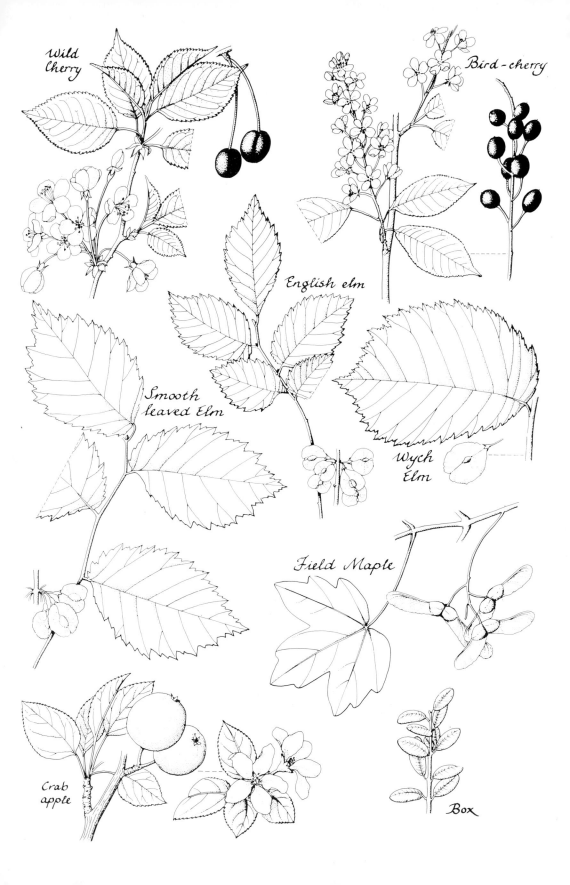

Wild Cherry

Bird-cherry

English elm

Smooth leaved Elm

Wych Elm

Field Maple

Crab apple

Box

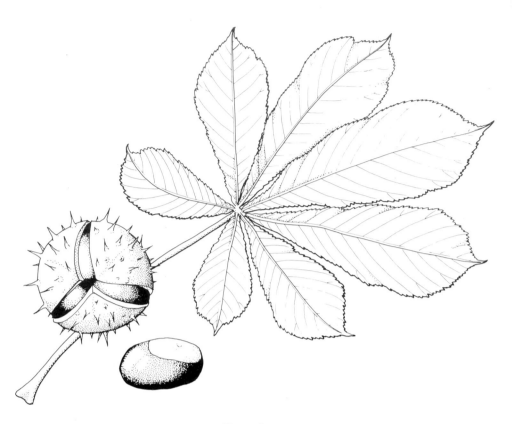

Horse chestnut

The horse chestnut, *Aesculus hippocastanum* L., was probably introduced later than the sweet chestnut and it has not become naturalised. The closest true habitat for it is in the Balkans. British horse chestnuts have all been planted.

Sweet chestnut prefers an acid soil and – although individual trees can be found growing on many soils – it is only on these that stands occur. The trees themselves increase the acidity until it reaches the level they prefer. Such soils tend to be sandy or silty, though a range of acid soils will support sweet chestnuts, and consequently woods in which they occur may be of several distinct types. The differences between one and another are indicated by the trees that occur with the sweet chestnuts: lime or ash grow with them on less acid soils, but the most usual companions are hornbeam or oak, sometimes with birch growing alongside the hornbeam-sweet-chestnut stands.

Once established, the sweet chestnut is large, and produces a dense, spreading canopy that shades out most competitors. It grows rapidly, but is long-lived, and it regenerates rapidly, which is why it was popular for coppicing. Its seeds are large, but birds sometimes carry them long distances. They are produced as copiously as those of oak, suffer less from predation, and germinate readily. Sweet chestnut can shade out hornbeam, can dominate even standard oaks, and often competes successfully against beech and hazel.

The wood has the valuable property of durability even when it is in contact with the ground. It does not rot readily. Large sweet-chestnut timber is used for the floors of buildings, making furniture or wood-turning. Smaller coppice wood is used in estate work, and, because it cleaves easily, to make paling fences.

According to Oliver Rackham, it now has a definite ecological role in East Anglian woods and perhaps more widely in Britain, possibly in a succession that begins with lime, which is replaced by hornbeam and oak, and ends with sweet chestnut.

Woods containing sweet chestnut may be found throughout most of Britain, but sweet-chestnut woodland occurs most commonly in the south-east of England. Good examples of it can be seen in several places.

Essex: Blakes Wood nature reserve, Copperas Wood nature reserve, and Stour Wood.
Kent: Blean Woods National Nature Reserve, Ham Street Woods National Nature Reserve, Flatroper's Wood nature reserve, Denge Wood, and Park Wood.
Surrey: Nower Wood nature reserve.
Sussex: Guestling Wood.

Crab Apple (*Malus sylvestris* (L.) Mill.)
The wild apple is the species which still supplies the rootstock for all cultivated apples. It is generally accepted as being native, but according to Sir Harry Godwin (see Further Reading) all the earliest records of it are from archaeological sites. Probably it was brought to Britain in neolithic times, although it is impossible to say when the cultivation of apples began. They used to be dried and carried about, so the remains of seeds and cultivated fruit found at some archaeological sites may have been imported. Probably wild crab-apples were gathered for food in large quantities.

By the Middle Ages, crab-apple trees were established over most of the country. They were fully naturalised, and grew in hedgerows and in most kinds of woodland, but always as isolated trees, for they do not form stands. Those you find today may be escapes from cultivation.

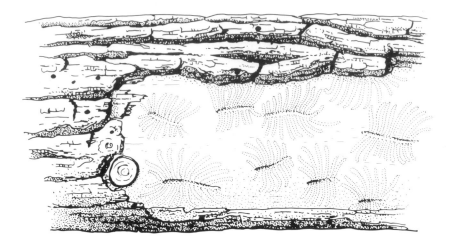

The channels left through elm bark and under it by the beetles that spread Dutch elm disease

Elm (*Ulmus* L. species)

One of Britain's most handsome and, until its large numbers were ravaged by Dutch elm disease, most conspicuous trees because of its frequent occurrence in hedgerows. The disease has made the elm a topic of conversation, a cause for concern, the subject of letters to newspapers. To botanists, the debate surrounding it is not new; it has always been a controversial genus, and its numbers have fluctuated widely in the past. This current epidemic is not even the first serious outbreak of Dutch elm disease.

Elms have grown in Britain, usually sparsely, since about 2 million years ago, disappearing during glaciations and returning in the interglacials. It is not certain when they entered the country during the present interglacial. Pollen has been found and dated as about 9,000 years old, but it may have been carried by winds from the south. Almost certainly the elm grew here more than 8,000 years ago, and soon after that it began to increase dramatically; in southern England and Ireland it became the most common tree. Then, about 5,000 years ago, the elm declined rapidly over most of Europe; in no more than about 500 years its numbers halved.

In historical times, elms were found mainly in hedgerows, but there were also elm woodlands. In modern times, however, Dutch elm disease seems to have struck repeatedly. There is evidence of an epidemic in the 1820s, which lasted for about forty years, and the disease was widespread in Britain for most of this century prior to the outbreak beginning in the late 1960s. Elm is very prone to fungal invasion, to bacterial infection, and to physical damage by insects that eat foliage and mammals that eat bark.

The earlier elm decline, in prehistoric times, remains un-explained. It is known that it occurred rapidly and simultaneously over a large area, and that only elms were affected. The most popular explanation, that early farmers destroyed vast numbers of elms, may not be the whole of the story. Modern cattle spend much of their time grazing, but left to themselves they revert readily to the habits of their ancestors, and vary their diet by browsing – eating the leaves of shrubs and such tree leaves as they can reach. Goats prefer browse to grass. It may be, therefore, that stalled animals were fed on leaves cut from the tops of trees which were pollarded for the purpose. This would not kill the trees, but it would reduce their production of pollen, and so the decline may have been of pollen rather than trees. Since the recorded history of our plants is based largely on the identification of pollen, which is preserved for very long periods, the 'elm decline' may be a product of the method of investigation, an artefact.

Alternatively, whole areas of forest, rich in elm because it was common everywhere, may have been cleared to provide pasture on which stock could be grazed. It has been suggested recently that beavers may have assisted in this operation. The lakes that form behind their dams can be extensive, and beavers use substantial quantities of wood in their construction, in the building of their lodges and as food. When the dam silts and the site must be abandoned, it will dry out slowly, or more rapidly if the dam is destroyed, and survives for a time as a grassy clearing in the woodland. Early farmers may have allowed their stock to graze this temporary pasture intensively, which would make the clearing permanent by destroying tree seedlings. Elm seedlings are parti-cularly liked by grazing animals, so might have been affected more seriously than other trees. At the same time, disease may have been affecting them: if natural regeneration was barely sufficient to balance the losses it caused, human inroads may have tipped the balance against the elms.

The final elm controversy concerns the species found here. What do we mean by 'elm'? Pollen produced by members of the genus *Ulmus* is easy to identify, but it is much more difficult to say from which elm species it came. Also there is disagreement about the classification of the species. Most elms reproduce vegetatively, rather than by growing from seed. Where stands of elm occur, it is likely that the trees are clones, all of them genetically identical, and grown from suckers thrusting up from the roots of adjacent trees. Yet in most years elms do produce seed, some of it germinates, and seedlings are not uncommon, though they tend not to survive. When they do, the great genetic variability of elms means they may appear to differ from their parents, and so may be accorded the taxonomic status of a species. The confusion is made worse by the readiness with which elm species hybridise with one another, and the large number of species which has been introduced and then hybridised.

The one elm that reproduces by seed regularly in Britain is *U. glabra* Huds., the wych-elm, and it seems likely that this was the first elm to establish itself here, and the one which was most abundant in the primeval forest. Today wych-elms occur most commonly in western and highland areas. The 'English' elm, *U. procera* Salisb., spreads by suckering. It grows best from the English Midlands south, and probably entered the country early in the Flandrian. It is at the northern limit of its geographical range, and at first may have been confined to the south and south-east of England. It is the species most prone to Dutch elm disease. The smooth-leaved elm, *U. minor* Mill. (or *carpinifolia* Gleditsch or Suckow), which also spreads by suckering, grows naturally only to the south and east of a line from the Humber to South Wales.

Wych-elm occurs widely in woodland in the north and west of Britain, but is less common in the east. There is an elm resembling it known as the 'lineage' elm, which in fact is intermediate between the wych and either the English or smooth-leaved elm; it may be a hybrid, although this is uncertain. Because of their readiness to hybridise, elms are evolving rapidly, and the lineage elm may well be an emerging species whose history began in Roman times or earlier, from the meeting of wych-elm with the English and smooth-leaved elms. If so, it will be sad if the evolutionary process is terminated through the combined effects of woodland clearance and disease, but this could happen.

Lineage elms prefer a slightly acid soil and can sometimes survive under quite acid conditions. They form pure stands, each stand being genetically different from the others. The trees themselves may be up to 6ft in diameter. You are most likely to find them in eastern England, in the company of sweet chestnut, hornbeam or lime. Unlike *U. procera* and *U. minor* they are not associated with the edge of woodland, and they have not invaded from hedgerows. Lineage elms sucker only weakly, however, and they are at risk from the disease. They have also suffered from decades of woodland clearance, and today the largest surviving stand of them is on land belonging to the Essex Naturalists' Trust.

It is the manner of reproduction that provides the most obvious distinguishing feature among types of woodland elm. If the trees occur singly, they are more likely to have grown from seed, and they will be wych-elm. If they occur in groups, probably they are reproducing vegetatively, and belong to one of the other two species, or are lineage elms.

Elms are among the most common of woodland trees, occurring in perhaps three-quarters of all woods. Two-thirds of the woodland elms are either *U. procera* or *U. minor*, which often form secondary woodland. They are very invasive and compete successfully with ash, field maple, hazel and even oak, especially where the oak is coppiced. The invasion begins at the edge of the wood, as elms there mature and send out suckers into the wood. These emerge, wait until the felling or coppicing of adjacent trees lets in light, then grow rapidly, overtaking the other underwood species. This establishes more mature elms, which send more suckers still further into the wood, and so the process is repeated. Of the two species whose clones invade in this way, smooth-leaved elm (*U. minor*) is the more aggressive, although where the dominant tree in the wood is hornbeam the invasion is more likely to be of English elm, *U. procera*.

Such invasion is most likely on clay soils which have a high pH, soils more fertile than those found in many woodlands. Birch also invades woodland in this way, but it is rare for both elm and birch to invade the same wood.

Woodland elms are less severely affected by Dutch elm disease than hedgerow elms. Although mature trees may be destroyed, their suckers often survive and so the trees may regenerate.

Elm had so many uses it is difficult to list them. It is an attractive timber, moderately strong: it has a twisted, crossed grain, meaning it has to be sawn, and will not split along the line of the grain; also it is very durable in water, provided it remains fully immersed. Traditionally it was used for making sea-defences and installations at sea ports, as well as for coffins, weatherboarding, chopping-blocks, farm carts, wheelbarrows, water-wheels, furniture, clogs and many ornamental items, as well as for the keels of ships and for water-pipes. Elm pipes laid beneath London in the seventeenth century and rediscovered earlier in this century were still sound.

You can see woodland wych-elm at Colerne Wood, in Wiltshire. Much of it here was destroyed by Dutch elm disease, but there is some regeneration.

Field maple (*Acer campestre* L.)
Field maples occur naturally over the whole of England and are especially common in the Midlands and south-east. They occur only

rarely, probably as an introduced species, in Scotland.

Although it grew here in the remote past, we have no record of it during the present interglacial before about 4,500 years ago. It arrived late in Britain, then, in neolithic times, and strictly speaking is not native, but by the Middle Ages field maples were among the most common of English trees. They are long-lived: individuals at least 300 years old are alive and well in the New Forest, and probably there are others of similar age elsewhere. Field maples have often been coppiced or pollarded, which may extend their life-span. They can dominate woodland, as in Hatfield Forest, or Milden Thicks in Suffolk, where they account for more than half the underwood. More usually they grow in association with ash and hazel.

The field maple casts a dense shade, and itself tolerates shade. It tends to prefer rather heavy, calcareous soils, and sometimes may be found on the more fertile sites in woods otherwise dominated by oak, hornbeam or sweet chestnut. Woods containing significant amounts of field maple occur in many parts of England. It is worth looking for it in any old wood, and if the wood has been coppiced in the past you may find coppiced stools of field maple. These may be large and there are said to be good examples in Hatfield Forest, just over the Essex border from Bishop's Stortford. Although common, it is close to its climatic limit in Britain. Its reproduction rate has fallen in modern times, possibly to a level too low to maintain it. Its small seedlings are uncommon and it fruits irregularly.

Its fine-grained, pale wood has been used to make snuff-boxes, pipes and other highly decorated items, and in Wales it used to be the preferred material for making drinking bowls called 'mazers', from which it gets its Welsh common name of *masarn*.

Hawthorn (*Crataegus* L. species)

A 'spinney' is a place where thorn trees ('spines') grow – and they grow almost anywhere. The earliest record of them in Britain dates from about 10,000 years ago, and by the time the first reference to them appears in the literature of these islands they had become associated with beliefs and legends that were already ancient and they had found their primary use.

The botanical generic name *Crataegus* comes from the Greek word *kratos*, meaning 'strength', partly in the sense of fortification, for at least since Roman times the hawthorn has been used to define boundaries. The hawthorn hedge is older than some people suppose. To the Greeks and Romans, though, hawthorn was sacred to Hymen, the god of marriage. This association transferred itself to our use of its flowers in May Day celebrations, which at one time were the fertility rites of spring. It was probably the rejection of the old beliefs by the simple expedient of standing them on their heads which led in Britain to the association of hawthorn with bad luck of any kind, so that people would not – some still will not – allow the delightful 'may' flowers into their houses. According to legend, hawthorn was used to make the crown of thorns worn by Jesus.

It is not all bad news, though. Another legend holds that Joseph of Arimathea visited Britain with twelve disciples, landing on the Isle of Avalon, near what is now Glastonbury. At the end of a long day the party could find no shelter and slept in the open, Joseph sticking his wooden staff into the ground. By morning the staff had produced roots and was in full flower. The disciples decided the miracle meant their travels should end, and they stayed to establish a church. The Glastonbury thorn, which according to legend still flowers at Christmas, is said to be that very hawthorn. More prosaically, it is a variety of hawthorn which flowers twice a year, in May and in January, and sometimes appears a bit early.

Hawthorn was certainly present in the wildwood and today it will invade unmanaged grassland at the least opportunity, eventually forming secondary woodland. This is most likely to appear where grazing pressure is reduced on abandoned grassland, and especially if there are few rabbits: when it is very young it is palatable to some animals, though when its spines harden it is very resistant to grazing. Once established, hawthorn trees are remarkably persistent, up to 25ft tall, forming a dense canopy and shading out all competition. They give way eventually, but hawthorn does not disappear completely, and individual trees can be found in almost all ancient woodlands.

There are two species of hawthorn: *C. monogyna* Jacq., which grows in hedgerows and is commoner, and *C. oxycanthoides* Thuill., the woodland or Midland hawthorn that grows throughout the south-east of England, extending into the Midlands. Both species will grow to tree size, although the woodland hawthorn is the smaller, and the two will hybridise.

C. monogyna is very invasive. The fruits of *C. monogyna* contain one seed, those of *C. oxycanthoides* two or three. The former can be found in woodland on all but the most acid soils, mainly in association with ash, field maple and hazel. In lime, hornbeam, oak and sweet-chestnut woods it may be found growing on the bank of earth that often forms the boundary. Woodland hawthorn occurs in much the same way within its geographical range, but is rather more tolerant of shade than *monogyna*.

Among the places where you can see hawthorn woodland is:
West Yorkshire: Hetchell Wood nature reserve.

Hazel (*Corylus avellana* L.)
The hazel is an old native of Britain. It has grown here during most of the recent interglacials and the ancestors of our present trees grew here 10,000 years ago, as the last glaciation was ending. Indeed, it may have been here even earlier. Its distribution suggests that it entered Britain from somewhere near the west coast of Scotland, spreading into north-eastern Ireland and north-western Great Britain. It is still more common in the north and west of England, Wales and Scotland than it is in the south and east. It is declining, however, possibly because squirrels and birds take too many of its nuts before they ripen, so inhibiting regeneration, although the burying of ripe nuts helps the tree. Nut production never was reliable, and although people too have enjoyed hazel nuts throughout history, as a crop they were of little economic significance.

The wood, on the other hand, has been important. The poles, or small branches, produced by coppicing were used to make baskets and hurdles; when thick enough they could make walking-sticks or broom-handles; even the inner bark was used, to make a twine.

Hazel grows mainly as an undershrub in woodland of many kinds, and although it cannot compete against taller trees, where it is unshaded and allowed to grow to its full size it can attain a height of 20ft or more. As a full-grown tree its pollen production increases, and it may be that the large amount of hazel pollen found in soils dated to the early stages of the interglacial came from pure hazel woodland.

Woodlands in which three-quarters or more of the underwood is hazel occur mainly on acid soils. In many parts of the country the purest stands are on infertile, acid, sand or loess soils. Where the soil is rather less acid and more fertile, hazel may be associated with field maple or sweet chestnut. If sand or loess overlie boulder clay, as they do in parts of Suffolk, the proportion of maple will be higher. Where the soil is of the boulder-clay type, ash may also be present, and there may be relatively less maple.

Hazel is one of the commonest of all woodland trees in the lowlands of England, and there are many hazel woods; but it is declining. Perhaps it is a relic of former climatic conditions, fated to disappear gradually from our countryside until it becomes rare. It can still be seen in most established woodland, and there are a few woods in which it is still widespread and important.

68

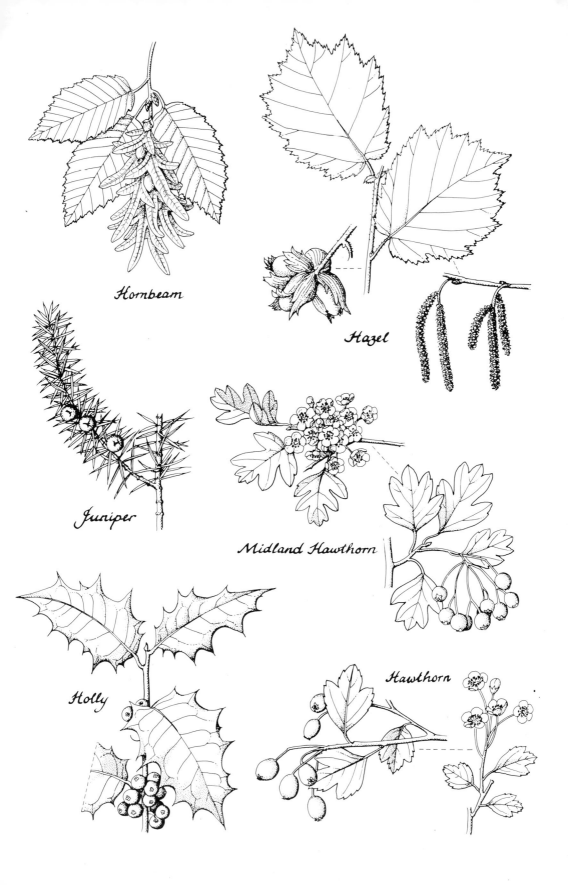

Hornbeam

Hazel

Juniper

Midland Hawthorn

Holly

Hawthorn

Cambridgeshire: Aversley Wood.
Devon: Shaptor Wood.
Dorset: Fifehead Wood and Horse Close Wood.
Kent: Park Wood.
Northamptonshire: Stoke Wood.

Holly (*Ilex aquifolium* L.)
Holly cannot tolerate hard frosts, too many of them kill it by damaging the cambium layer of the stem and branches, especially in seedlings. It is an excellent monitor of climatic change, as its wood and leaves tend to preserve well, it produces little pollen and its pollen is not carried far by the wind.

It arrived rather late in Britain, but was present in many places by about 8,000 years ago. In the succeeding millennia it became widespread and common, although its preference for an oceanic climate has always made it commoner in the west of the country than in the east.

The tree grows slowly, but once it is established it is difficult to kill. It can be coppiced or pollarded without being harmed, and its tenacity enabled it to survive repeated forest clearances by early 'slash-and-burn' farmers. They would clear-fell an area of woodland, set fire to such wood as they did not need for their immediate use, then graze their livestock on the grasses which grew in the clearing they had made. Many trees recover slowly from such treatment, and so tend to give way to more robust species if the grazing is often repeated. Holly survived the grazing, and indeed it spread along with primitive farming because of the unpalatability of its seedlings to livestock, and its apparent popularity among early farmers, who had uses for it and encouraged it. It makes excellent fuel, burning hot and fierce even when green. In a hard winter the farmers would collect holly leaves, crush them, and feed them to deer and other livestock; the animals would not eat it from choice, but it provided some kind of winter feed when all else failed.

It occurs today in hedgerows and in many kinds of woodland, though it seems to favour oakwoods. Usually it is an understorey tree, but it can grow to a height of 80ft or more. It is most common on acid soils, tolerating very acid conditions, and improving them by forming humus and reducing the acidity. It is found occasionally on calcareous soils, and is generally increasing.

Woods dominated by stands of holly may be peculiar to Britain and are a rare example of broadleaved evergreen forest extending into the higher temperate latitudes. In some cases the holly stands may be part of a succession that will lead to beech or oak woodland, but there are instances of it becoming truly dominant and killing out established oaks. The most famous holly woods are in the New Forest, at Dungeness, Stiperstones Forest in Shrophire, in Epping Forest, and at Staverton Park, Suffolk, which is said to have the most impressive of all holly stands. A holly wood produces a dense, complete canopy, and little grows beneath it except bryophytes.

Hornbeam (*Carpinus betulus* L.)

A tree of continents, intolerant of the spring frosts which occur more often in oceanic than in continental climates, hornbeam grows naturally only in the south-east of England. Where it does grow, however, it may be very common, since it tends to form pure stands. It entered Britain during several earlier interglacials, but became fully established only at a fairly late stage. In the present interglacial it was probably here, but very local, by about 8,000 years ago, or possibly a little earlier; it was still not common as recently as 3,000 years ago.

It has been managed in the past to produce firewood, but its hard timber now has little value, although it was formerly used to make piano keys, butchers' blocks, cog-wheels and axles for carts. Though it yields nothing edible, it seems to follow humans – perhaps because it is intolerant of shade, and its seedlings are likely to thrive only if nearby competition is reduced through coppicing or felling. At the same time it is highly resistant to grazing and cutting, and regenerates rapidly. Thus forest clearance actually helped it. As former forest land was abandoned by farmers, it flourished in the absence of its main competitors. It has always flourished when wars have driven farmers from their land, although this slightly sinister opportunism seems not to have generated legends.

In modern times it has been planted widely in the south and east of the country as a park tree, and in cities, especially in London. It occurs in wood-pasture, which is open woodland in which livestock graze, but it is just as likely to be found in pure hornbeam woods and in mixed woodland, where it may associate with field maple, ash, or oak.

Hornbeam will grow on most soils, provided there is at least some clay, but it seems to show a slight preference for mildly acid conditions. Its seeds, produced abundantly in some years, germinate well. It is not invasive, although it can appear in secondary woodland following the first felling. It has been planted in many woods, especially around the edges.

At the north-western edge of its natural range, in north Hertford-

71

shire, hornbeam grows in association with field maple, or field maple and hazel, on rather heavy, acid, boulder clay. In East Anglia it is more usually found growing with ash, on lighter soils. Further south, in parts of Essex and in south Hertfordshire, it grows beside oak, or, more rarely, in pure hornbeam woods.

Where it occurs with oak it is possible, but far from certain, that the hornbeam forms part of a succession toward oak woodland and eventually will disappear. It is uncertain because there is at least one wood, Wormley Wood, Hertfordshire, in which the hornbeam may be replacing the oak, and so the succession that seems natural may in fact be due to past management which encouraged oak. In general, hornbeam seems to have replaced lime, although the reasons are not clear. Or it could be that, like beech, hornbeam is still extending its range in response to climatic change.

That said, it is sad to have to report that in the last forty years something like one-third of all the hornbeam woodlands in Britain have been felled. They can still be seen in a few places.

Hertfordshire: Wormley Wood, where hornbeam grows with oak.
Kent: Denge Wood, where hornbeam grows with sweet chestnut and yew.

Juniper (*Juniperus communis* L.)
Strictly speaking, juniper is a shrub rather than a tree, although it can grow to a height of more than 12ft. Interestingly, in Britain it is a relic of the last glaciation, for it is truly a plant of the tundra. It grew here in the late Devensian, and was common and widespread at the start of the Flandrian interglacial. As the climate became warmer, so the juniper retreated, but not because it demanded cooler conditions. Indeed, at first it responded to warmth by growing larger and producing more pollen. What it could not tolerate was the shade cast by the invading birch. Bitter cold and deep snow might stunt its growth, but it was the shade which finally drove it to those places where it thrives today.

You can see this history stage by stage if you find a place where juniper grows on a slope and follow it up the hill. At the bottom, if the site is fairly open, it will be a small tree. As you move higher the trees will be smaller until they are shrubs and at the top you will find only low bushes. At one time juniper grew in this way on Juniper Hill, at Mickleham on the North Downs in Surrey. Do junipers grow yet on Juniper Hill?

It can be found growing on chalk and limestone in southern England, in northern Scotland and the Lake District, on high heaths and moors, above the tree line in mountains, but also, sometimes, in birch and pine woods. Outside Britain it extends far into the Arctic. When it was common it is believed to have done much to stabilise and improve soils.

It also achieved immortality of a kind by flavouring gin and giving its name to it: *Genièvre* is the French for 'juniper', and 'gin', made with the help of juniper berries, is a corruption of the French word. In Scandinavia, though, juniper berries are used to flavour meats.

Lime or linden (*Tilia* L. species)

About 6,000 years ago, lime was probably the commonest tree over much of southern and eastern England. It seems to have been far commoner than either elm or oak, giving way only to alder on the wetter ground. This is said with some caution because the pollen record may have given a misleading impression: lime produces large amounts of extremely durable and easily identifiable pollen, which could have led to over-representation. On the other hand, the flowers are pollinated by insects and the amount of pollen released into the air is fairly small. It is pollen in the air that falls to the surface, to be trapped in peat and so stored. This may mean lime is under-represented in the pollen record.

Lime entered Britain about 9,000 years ago, but it spread only slowly to the north and west, was never common in Wales and may not have penetrated Scotland and Ireland at all. Then it declined, in neolithic times and in the Bronze Age, always to be replaced by grass. The decline was due to forest clearance by farmers, at least on low ground. Lime rarely sets viable seed in Britain, so that once removed from an area it is difficult for it to return. Its decline in the uplands is more difficult to explain.

There are two species native to Britain: small-leaved lime (*T. cordata* Mill.), which used to be the commoner, and large-leaved lime (*T. platyphyllos* Scop.), which demands more warmth and grows naturally only locally in Britain. You may find it in South Wales, the Welsh Marches and the north Midlands. The most common lime tree today is *T. vulgaris* Hayne, a hybrid of the two native species, which has been planted extensively since the late seventeenth century. All limes are long-lived, and there are individuals alive now which may be more than 300 years old. Those in St James's Park, London, are supposed to have been planted around 1660 at the suggestion of John Evelyn.

Where *T. cordata* occurs in woods, those woods probably date from medieval times or earlier. Planted lime woodlands are much more recent and consist almost wholly of *T. vulgaris*.

Limes are not invasive, but they can thrive on a variety of soils, including poorly drained ones that might discourage other trees, apart from the alders with which they often keep company. They tend to occur as pure stands formed as clones, often adjacent to woodland dominated by hornbeam or ash, or more rarely oak or sweet chestnut. On more fertile soils, small stands of limes may be found close to field maple or elm. There are lime-oak woodlands, similar in formation in many ways to hornbeam-oak woodlands.

Lime trees are distributed patchily in Britain and can be found most easily in particular, scattered areas on the Suffolk–Essex border, the Bedfordshire–Cambridgeshire border, in Norfolk, Lincolnshire, Derbyshire, the Lake District, part of the Wye Valley and in the Mendip Hills in Somerset. They are gregarious trees, confined almost wholly to woodlands. Where isolated trees occur in hedgerows usually this is because the hedgerows themselves are the remains of former woodland.

It is uncommon for lime to establish itself from seed in this country. Its seedlings are intolerant of shade, and the mature trees cast a dense shade. Occasionally a seedling will succeed, and this may account for the presence of limes in secondary woodland, but in general lime is able to maintain itself only in sites it has occupied for centuries, and does not colonise new areas.

Its wood has never been particularly popular, but it did have some uses and users. Grinling Gibbons (1648–1721) used it for his carvings, including that of a frieze of flowers which can still be seen in St Paul's Church, Covent Garden, London, and it was used to make musical instruments. Mostly, though, it has been used to feed livestock or just for decoration.

To many people who park their cars beneath them, limes are best known for the honeydew they appear to secrete so profusely as sticky drops that set quite hard. Its presence would be noted at once by any good herdsman, as indicating that the foliage is rich in sugars. Perhaps it was the honeydew that first attracted the early stockmen to it. In fact it is not produced by the tree at all, but by aphids, sap-suckers that pierce the outer tissues of leaves and stems to feed on the sap. They need to obtain sugars from it, of course, to give them the energy to go on sucking, but they also need proteins and minerals, and sweet sap is rather deficient in these. The aphids get round the problem by consuming vast quantities of sap, extracting the nutrients they need, and excreting the surplus. In order to obtain enough minerals and proteins they have to get rid of much surplus sugar, and that is what they excrete, as honeydew.

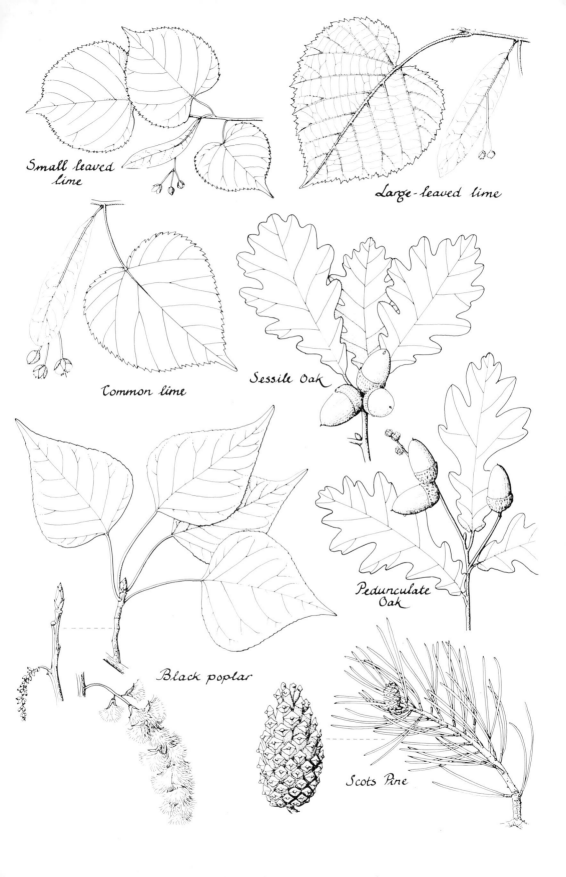

Small leaved
lime

Large-leaved lime

Common lime

Sessile Oak

Pedunculate
Oak

Black poplar

Scots Pine

The sticky drops, then, are aphid droppings. Next time they coat the car, blame the bugs, not the tree! Limes are not the only plants from which honeydew is produced, of course. There are many, but we do not line streets with them as often as with limes.

You can see lime woodland in just a few places.

Lincolnshire: Hatton Wood, in Bardney Forest National Nature Reserve.
Suffolk: Groton Wood nature reserve.

Oak (*Quercus* L. species)

As the Devensian glaciers retreated, the most 'English' of trees was advancing across continental Europe. Its pollen, carried ahead of it by the wind, was reaching Britain in substantial amounts from about 12,000 years ago. Probably it was growing locally in southern England by 10,000 years ago, and by 7,000 years ago it was established over the whole country – an important component of the wildwood. But oak woods were confined to the uplands. In the lowlands oaks may have been dominant very locally, within the surrounding wildwood, or they may have existed as scattered individuals. In some places they were rare, in others they were the second most common tree. The importance of oak has been overestimated by people who have called any wood containing oak an oak wood.

Two species of oak grew in the original wildwood, common or pedunculate oak (*Q. robur* L.), and sessile or durmast oak (*Q. petraea* (Mattuschka) Liebl.). Paradoxically, sessile oak was the more common. Today sessile oak is usually confined to valley bottoms or other low ground, although in a few places it is the only oak. There is sessile oak woodland on the Lizard Peninsula in Cornwall, and in some places on Dartmoor, for example at Wistman's Wood. It is the more common of the two species locally in parts of northern Scotland. The holm or evergreen oak (*Q. ilex* L.) is really a Mediterranean species, which must have been introduced to Britain, probably early in the Iron Age.

Today oak is the commonest of all British native trees. Where stands of oak occur they indicate either an invasion – usually of pedunculate oak – of abandoned waste or farm land, or woodlands of some antiquity. Oak also occurs in wood-pasture, especially in the New Forest, Forest of Dean, Wyre Forest and Sherwood Forest, possibly because it can withstand grazing better than its competitors. Its seedlings are unpalatable to livestock, and the oak has a tap-root weighing up to three times more than the part of the tree

76

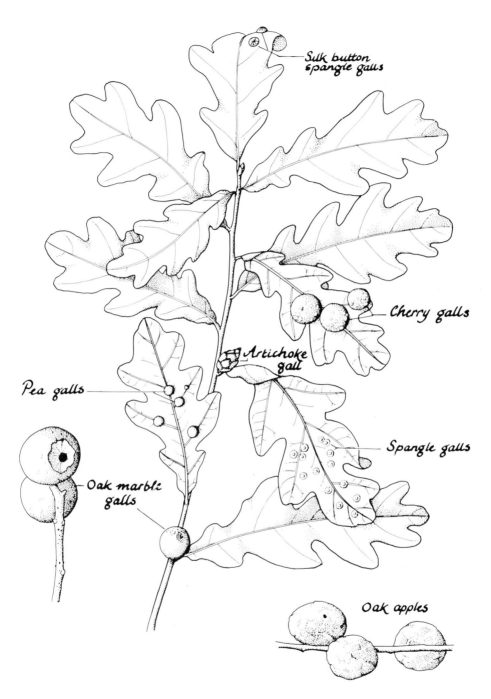

Silk button
spangle galls

Cherry galls

Artichoke
gall

Pea galls

Spangle galls

Oak marble
galls

Oak apples

Common oak galls

showing above ground, so there are ample nutrient reserves available for the repair of any damage that does occur.

Oak woods, in which sessile oak is the more common species, occur on soils containing little clay. Oaks produce very acid conditions in the soil around them, and oak woods have soils more acid than those of any other wood. This limits the species which can grow near them, although you find oak growing with other trees, most commonly in the company of birch, hornbeam, sweet chestnut, holly or rowan. All of these are able to grow on poor soils. Oak woods occur in both highlands and lowlands, but they are much more common in the highlands and in the west of Britain. Oaks are very common in secondary woodland, in plantations and in hedgerows.

The wood of the oak is handsome, hard and durable. The heartwood withstands prolonged immersion in fresh or salt water, and was used to build sea-defences. Traditionally it has been used for building, making barges and railway wagons, for furniture, coffins and barrels. In the past the tree was planted for more than just its timber: its bark was used for tanning, and of course bark can be obtained only from trees that have been felled.

Oaks are parasitised by many species of gall-producing insects, most of them wasps so small they are difficult to see with the naked eye, and in 1830 one species of gall wasp, *Andricus kollari*, was introduced deliberately for the purpose. It produces oak marble galls on pedunculate oak. The galls contain female wasps which emerge in spring and their complex life-cycle continues with the production of 'ant-pupae' galls on Turkey oak (*Q. cerris* L.), a species that was introduced but is now fairly well naturalised in many parts of Britain. The wasp needs the Turkey oak, but the dyeing and ink industry, which was responsible for introducing the wasp, needed the oak marble galls. They contain 17 per cent by dry weight of tannic acid, and were used to make blue-black ink.

Oak woods have been in decline for more than a century, as the trees are failing to regenerate. This may be due partly to the cessation of traditional forms of management, especially of coppicing. Oak seedlings are intolerant of shade. Among coppiced trees they had time to establish themselves before the mature trees regenerated and shaded them, but beneath a canopy that is more or less closed they are at a grave disadvantage. In the wildwood it is likely that oak seedlings survived only in clearings formed by the death and fall of old trees. There may be increased predation of acorns by small mammals, which would exacerbate the problem by reducing the number of seedlings which are struggling to become established.

You can see good examples of oak woodland in many places.

Cambridgeshire: Hayley Wood nature reserve.
Clwyd: Bigwood, where it grows with ash.
Cornwall: Lavethan Wood.
Derbyshire: Ladybower Wood nature reserve.
Devon: Yarner Wood National Nature Reserve, Wistman's Wood nature reserve, Avon Wood, Buck's and Keivell's Woods and Shaptor Wood.
Dyfed: Coed Rheidol National Nature Reserve.
Grampian Region: Dinnet Oakwood National Nature Reserve.
Gwynedd: Coed y Rhygen National Nature Reserve, Coed Allt and Coed Lletywalter.
Hereford and Worcester: Wyre Forest National Nature Reserve and Chaddesey National Nature Reserve.
Hertfordshire: Hoddesdonpark Wood, and Wormley Wood where it grows with hornbeam.
Highland Region: Loch Sunart Woodlands National Nature Reserve.
Kent: Blean Woods National Nature Reserve and Ham Street Woods National Nature Reserve.
Norfolk: Wayland Wood nature reserve.
Northumberland: Holystone Burn nature reserve and Holystone North Wood nature reserve.
Powys: Nant Irfon National Nature Reserve and Graig Wood.

Pear (*Pyrus* L. species)
The wild pear has grown in southern England since neolithic times. No one knows whether originally it was introduced by humans, but since the little fruit it produces cannot be eaten it probably arrived of its own accord. It was rare by the Middle Ages and now must be very rare indeed, a few isolated trees probably surviving in medieval woodlands, woodland edges and hedgerows. Nevertheless, the wild 'common' pear (*P. communis* L.) is the ancestor of all cultivated pears.

Plums (*Prunus* L. species)
Prunus species, such as *P. domestica* L., these days with many subspecies and varieties, the cultivated plum or damson, and *P. cerasus* L., the sour cherry, were introduced to Britain, long ago. They were being grown here during the Iron Age, and certainly by the Romans.

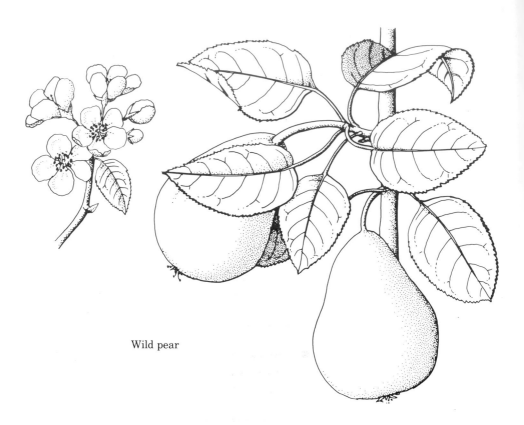

Wild pear

Poplar (*Populus* L. species)
A close relative of the aspen (*P. tremula*), but larger, the black
poplar or downy black poplar (*P. nigra* L. var. *betulifolia* (Pursh)
Torr.) was growing in Britain around 4,000 years ago in neolithic
times, and it may be native although this is not certain. According
to Rackham (*Trees and Woodland in the British Landscape*), in
documents written before 1650 the word 'poplar' apparently refers
to black poplar, which was then very common in some places.

It is a distinctive tree, often tall and thick, with a trunk that
usually leans, and curved branches. It grows on wet ground, often
beside rivers, and in woodland where there are conditions to suit it.

The white poplar or abele (*P. alba* L.) is usually believed to have
been introduced, although there is doubt about this too. References
to it in documents from the thirteenth and fourteenth centuries
imply that if it was introduced it was done a long time ago
(Rackham); the tree may actually be native.

Native or not, it was sacred to Hercules: according to the old
stories he used to wear a crown made from its leaves, and when
Cerberus dragged him off to the underworld he was still wearing

this wreath. When he emerged the leaves were blackened on the upper side but on the under side they had been bleached white by his sweat; this is why the white poplar's leaves are pale on the under side. The black poplar's leaves are dark on both sides.

The white, clean-looking wood is easy to work and has been used to make boxes, baskets ('chips') and matches.

The status of the grey poplar (*P. canescens* (Ait.) Sm.) used to be no less uncertain, but now it is known to be a hybrid between white poplar and aspen, and naturalised in some places.

Apart from these, various ornamentals have been planted in modern times. The Lombardy poplar is a variety of black poplar (*P. nigra*) propagated by cuttings taken originally in the eighteenth century from a tree in northern Italy. All Lombardy poplars are cloned from the original Italian tree.

Rowan or mountain ash (*Sorbus aucuparia* L.)
This tree of high northern latitudes entered Britain late in the Devensian glaciation, and as the climate improved it tended to be restricted to upland areas and to the north of the country. It is the commonest tree in the birch forests of Scotland – other than birch itself – and grows as an isolated tree wherever it can find a site protected from grazing. Further south it can be found in oak woods. It is also a tree of secondary woodland.

It occurs on poor, acid soils, and its ability to grow readily from seed may be causing it to become more common, especially in the lowlands.

Scots pine (*Pinus sylvestris* L. subspecies *scotia* (Schott) E.F. Warb.)
The true Scots pine is perhaps the most ancient of all British trees. It has grown here for the last 1 to 2 million years, disappearing only during the most severe glacial episodes and returning when conditions improved. In the present interglacial it was widespread and well established throughout the country by 10,000 years ago, being particularly common in south-east England. It spread north, and by about 7,000 years ago had colonised what was to become the Caledonian Forest of Scotland. Then it declined, as broadleaved species invaded, so that by 4,000 years ago it was much less common. The history of the tree is well documented because it tends to grow close to peat bogs, in which its remains are preserved.

It is very susceptible to fire, reproduces only from seed, does not regenerate readily following clearance, and is intolerant of shade. For these reasons it is displaced rather easily. However, it is very tolerant of poor soils, and forms secondary woodland readily.

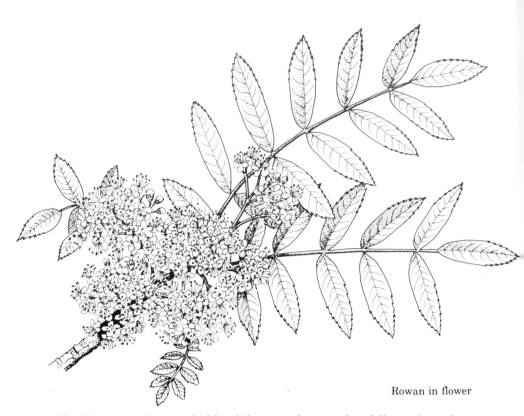

Rowan in flower

Neolithic peoples probably did not select it for felling, but they cleared it along with other species as part of the general forest clearance and had many uses for its timber. Today relics of the old pine woods remain in isolated parts of Scotland, at Rothiemurchus in the Cairngorms, for example, and around Lochs Maree and Rannoch; but the most impressive of them is the Glen Affric Forest.

Scots pine is used for all kinds of carpentry, but its principal commercial value derives from its height and the straightness of its stem. It used to provide masts and spars for ships, and it still provides pit props and telegraph poles. It was also used for railway sleepers when these were made of timber. It is the second most important softwood timber tree in Britain, and has been planted extensively in commercial woodlands.

Its wood is also imported in large amounts, usually under the name 'fir' or 'redwood'. The modern plantation trees are descended from imported stock, however, and although they have hybridised with *scotica* in some places neither they nor the hybrids are quite like *scotica*. The difference shows best when the trees are old: the original Scots pine retains its pyramid shape for a long time and then develops a round crown; the plantation varieties develop a flat crown, and develop it earlier in their lives. Scots pine, in one or other of its forms, is the most common conifer in Europe and grows throughout the temperate Old World.

It is very similar to lodgepole pine (*P. contorta* Dougl. ex Loud. var. *latifolia* S. Wats.), the inland representative of the shore pine of the west coast of North America, which has been planted in Britain commercially in modern times, and to Corsican pine (*P. nigra* var. *maritima* (Ait.) Melville), which has been grown in Britain for much longer than lodgepole pine. It is also more widely distributed, although these days it may not be the more numerous of the two because of the extent of lodgepole plantations. But there are other *Pinus* species that were introduced many centuries ago. The stone pine (*P. pinea* L.), for example, is believed to have been planted here by the Romans, who used its wood as an altar fuel.

Woodland dominated by Scots pine can still be seen in some places, although relics of original Scots pine woodland are found only in the Scottish Highlands. Elsewhere, even on nature reserves, the trees were planted fairly recently or have invaded abandoned open land. Much of the Scots pine in southern England has invaded naturally, as for example on the heathlands of Hampshire and Surrey.

Highland Region: Beinn Eighe National Nature Reserve and Glen Affric National Nature Reserve.
Norfolk: East Wretham Heath nature reserve and Thetford Heath National Nature Reserve.
Tayside Region: Rannoch Forest National Nature Reserve.

Sycamore (*Acer pseudoplatanus* L.)
This relative of the field maple (known in Scotland as the 'plane', not to be confused with the unrelated *Platanus acerifolia* Ait., the London plane) was brought to Britain from central Europe, probably in the fifteenth or sixteenth century. By the end of that time specimens had been planted, but the tree was still rare. It became more popular in the latter part of the eighteenth century and was planted more extensively. During the nineteenth century it expanded to form secondary woodland in highland areas where trees had been felled. Clearly it had become fully naturalised.

It reproduces by seed, and its seedlings are resistant to grazing. Tolerant of poor soils, it forms secondary woodland very readily, although it is still commoner outside woodland than within it. Sycamore woodland occurs most commonly on acid soils. It will invade mature climax woodland and in some places has become a troublesome weed. Deer find its bark edible, and this may limit its spread. It is common everywhere, but more so in the west of Britain than elsewhere.

Sycamore can be coppiced, and it has been planted widely in Scotland where it is a valuable timber tree. Its wood is often attractive, a clean-looking white, and apart from a tendency to split it works and finishes well and is easily treated with wood preservatives. Indoors it is hard and strong, which together with the smooth surface that can be given to it has made it popular for building dance-floors. As well as being very smooth it scrubs well, so it is used for cooking utensils and, until stainless-steel sink units became fashionable, was used to make draining-boards. It takes stain well and is used to make furniture, and for veneers. The wood has no odour and does not stain fabrics, so it was the preferred wood for making the rollers of mangles and much of the wooden equipment used in the textile industry.

Sycamore's winged seeds

Whitebeam (*Sorbus aria* (L.) Crantz)
A tree that grows up to 80ft tall, the whitebeam produces bright red berries, similar to those of its relative the rowan. It is native to Britain, although there are few pre-neolithic traces of it so perhaps it was scarce. Today it is widespread, although more common locally in southern England, where it takes the place of the rowan, than elsewhere. It occurs in woodland, especially in secondary woodland, often near the edge, but is confined to chalk and limestone soils.

It used to be coppiced to produce stakes and fuel, but is now planted only for ornament, and especially in towns because it is very tolerant of smoke.

Wild service (*Sorbus torminalis* (L.) Crantz)
Another relative of the rowan, and known in some parts of the country as the chequers tree, the wild service produces a brown fruit which is edible once it becomes over-ripe, or after a frost, and from which a fermented drink can be made.

It grew in Britain during earlier interglacials, but in the present one it is known only from the late Iron Age, although it is accepted as native. It can be found as a solitary tree in wood-pastures or woods, and sometimes occurs in hedges as far north as the Lake District. It can grow to a large size.

The 'wild' in its name is used to distinguish it from an exotic service tree (*S. domestica* L.) which has been planted occasionally for ornament. The wild service has never been of any commercial value and probably no one has bothered to plant it. Where it grows, therefore, its presence suggests ancient woodland that has remained undisturbed.

Willow (*Salix* species L.)
The common osier (*S. viminalis* L.), seen usually as a shrub but capable of developing into a tree 30ft tall, has grown in Britain for the last 42,000 years. It formed part of the tundra vegetation during the Devensian glaciation. It is one of about fifteen species of *Salix* which have grown here since the end of the glaciation or since early in the present Flandrian interglacial.

White willow (*S. alba* L.) and crack willow (*S. fragilis* L.) used to be planted beside rivers, and willows and sallows (also species of *Salix*) were commonly coppiced or pollarded. They were used for wickerwork and the making of many small wooden articles such as clothes-pegs and floats for anglers. They provided the material for the Easter palms, handed out in churches, and their seeds were used to stuff mattresses and pillows.

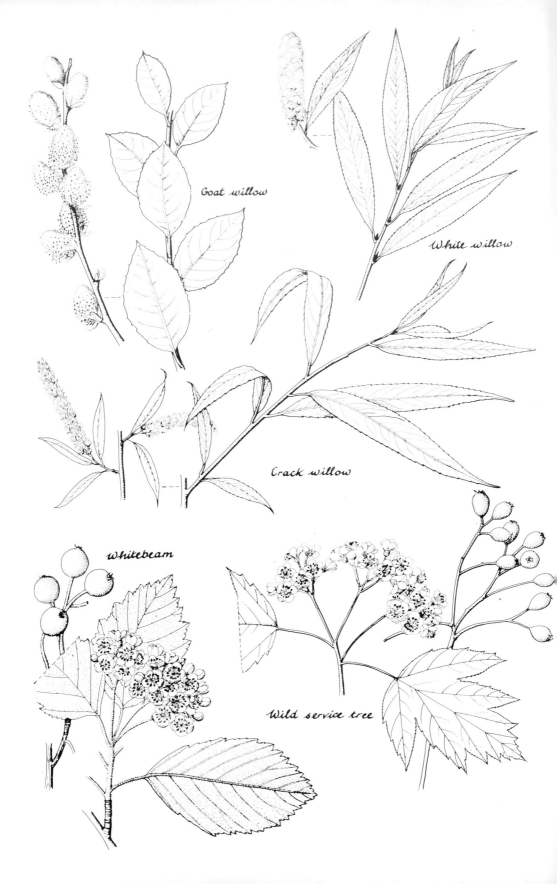

Goat willow

White willow

Crack willow

Whitebeam

Wild service tree

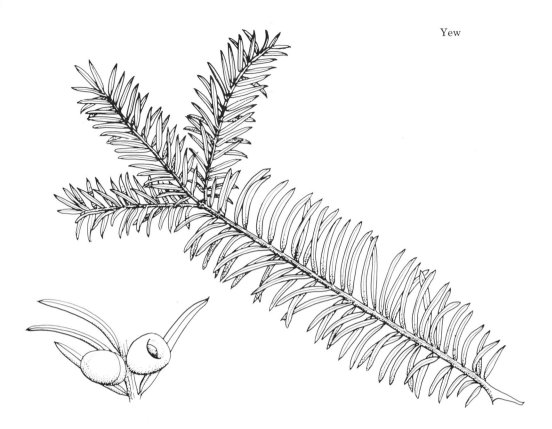

Most willows are not trees of woodland, preferring wet habitats; they are common on river banks and in hedgerows beside ditches. But those which can tolerate drier conditions occur sometimes in woods: you may find goat willow or great sallow (*S. caprea* L.) there, or common sallow (*S. cinerea* L.).

Apart from these, the other British willows and sallows include eared sallow (*S. aurita* L.), tea-leaved sallow (*S. phylicifolia* L.), creeping willow (*S. repens* L.), downy willow (*S. lapponum* L), woolly willow (*S. lanata* L.), and least willow (*S. herbacea* L.). The weeping willow (*S. babylonica* L.) is not native to Britain and is not very hardy anywhere in Europe; probably it was introduced from Iran.

Yew (*Taxus baccata* L.)
The yew is associated with churchyards, probably surviving in them today because they provide sanctuary for it: elsewhere it has been persecuted by farmers with livestock, because all parts of it except for the berries, but including the seeds, are extremely poisonous to mammals. It was originally planted in churchyards because in pre-

Christian times it was used in various occult rituals, and people believed it would purge a graveyard of lurking and unfriendly spirits. Symbolically, too, the evergreen yew is said to remind us of eternal life.

In the Middle Ages it was planted extensively, by then perhaps for more prosaic reasons. Its wood is hard, and nowadays very valuable. The oldest wooden man-made object in the world, a spear found in Essex, was made from yew 13,000 years ago. It was yew from which the longbow was made, and in North America it was the preferred material for Indian bows. The 'English' longbows used at Agincourt were invented in Wales, not England, and were made from imported yew, because the English variety was of inferior quality.

Yew is intolerant of severe and prolonged frost, and so it reached Britain late in the interglacial. Apart from the Essex spear the oldest traces of it date to about 8,000 years ago and it reached its maximum about 4,000 years ago. It can grow over the whole country as far north as the southern edge of the Scottish Highlands, but prefers a calcareous soil and a sheltered site. It used to grow in alder and birch woods in the fenlands, and in beech woods, but at one time yew woodlands may have been common. They occur on chalk and limestone soils and you can still find patches of yew woodland in southern England, and in Derbyshire, Cumbria, on the Welsh border, in Lincolnshire, and in East Anglia. We recommend the examples listed below.

Hereford and Worcester: Nupend Wood nature reserve.
Kent: Denge Wood and Park Wood.
Nottinghamshire: Hannah Wood, where it grows with beech.
West Sussex: Kingley Vale National Nature Reserve, which contains what is said to be the most impressive pure stand surviving today.

5
Clearing the Wildwood

Bird-cherry

Humans began to affect the primeval forest from the moment they arrived in Britain. As remarked earlier, all species modify their environments. They came, those pre-agricultural peoples, to make a living by hunting game and gathering food-plants. There were not many of them, and they wrought only minor changes: they made temporary clearings in which to build their shelters, and no doubt they set fire to anything that would burn, mainly in order to drive game into ambushes. If repeated, forest fires encourage the growth of tree species which can regenerate quickly, and the fires may have reduced the number of pines.

Greater change occurred about 5,000 years ago, when herbivorous animals had been domesticated, and their human owners had to find food for them. Confined in particular areas and more or less protected from predators, livestock populations must have increased. Most animals had to be killed each autumn, as the food supply dwindled, leaving only a nucleus from which the herds and flocks could increase again in the spring.

In the wild, cattle browse as well as graze, using the food supply economically. During spring and summer they rely mainly on such leaves as they can reach; in autumn and winter, when trees and shrubs are bare, they feed on the grass, which by then has grown tall. The early farmers sought to observe this feeding regime, but if they were keeping a large number of animals they had to supplement the local browse. So they climbed trees and stripped away the twigs bearing succulent young leaves. They seem to have preferred elm for this purpose, and to have gathered its twigs and leaves in such large amounts that the trees were prevented from flowering – and therefore from producing seed. Elms failed to reproduce fast enough to maintain their own numbers. As suggested

89

earlier, the process may have been aided by the activities of beavers. They had their own ways of clearing small areas of woodland, leading eventually to the formation of meadow, in which grazing would have restricted the regeneration of trees generally – and of elms especially, because of their palatability to animals. The involvement of humans in the elm decline is confirmed by the simultaneous growth of herbs such as stinging nettle and plantains, which are opportunists always associated with the disturbance of land by humans. The early farmers probably used lime trees in the same way, and may also have felled them for their timber and bark, for which they had many uses.

When farmers began to cultivate the land for plant crops, perhaps 2,500 years ago, the rate of change accelerated. Trees were felled, and probably fired where they lay. Livestock were allowed to graze in order to subdue regeneration from tree stumps, and the land was ploughed. The Celtic plough, which came to Britain around that time, made only a slight, shallow furrow, but the land was cross-ploughed, with two passes at right angles to one another; it worked well enough. It was the type of cultivation the Romans found when they came to Britain. But crop farming was still only local, and so were its effects on the forest.

Management of this kind may convert particular areas from dense forest, with a complete canopy, to something more like parkland, with an open tree cover and grass growing abundantly on such exposed land as is not being tilled. Yet the alteration is not great. Only in certain places did the forest disappear entirely; in parts of East Anglia and the Breckland, and in coastal areas, especially on what was to become the 'machair' in the Hebrides, where blown sand covered exposed land and prevented tree regeneration.

The farming was of the 'landnam' type, and it is still practised in many parts of the world, especially in the tropics. An area would be clear-felled. That a large-scale operation of this kind was feasible for people equipped with only stone implements has been doubted, but in fact it is not so difficult as it may sound. The stone axes have been reconstructed and tested, and found to be quite effective; and not every tree had to be cut in order to fell it. Particular trees would be chosen for felling because their fall would bring down others; the technique worked particularly well on sloping land. The felled trees would be left long enough for the unwanted foliage to wilt and dry, then it would be fired. When the fire died, cereals would be grown in the ashes.

After a time the nutrients in the soil would be depleted, crop yields would begin to fall, and the farmers prepared to move to a new area, leaving the land they abandoned to be reclaimed by the forest. The system can be sustained indefinitely provided there is sufficient land available to the farmers, but in Britain it was limited. The farmers preferred higher, more open ground, and light soils they could work easily. From these the tree cover disappeared and never returned.

The farming also changed the composition of the forests. As seen above, elms and then limes were declining, but it may be that farmers felled them, especially where they grew on the more fertile land. From the first, though, trees were themselves the source of essential raw materials, and even as the land was cleared some of them were being managed to yield sustainable crops. Hazel was being coppiced in Somerset some 4,000 years ago, and other species may have been managed in this way as well. Pollarding seems to have begun at around the same time. In both cases the primary reason was usually to supply browse for livestock, with wooden

The twiggy-looking plants are hazel that had been coppiced in an oak-hazel wood in southern England. Coppicing allows sunlight to reach the ground and this favours the spring flowers typical of open woodland that give our countryside so much of its colour and charm (*M. Nimmo/Frank Lane Agency*)

poles as a useful byproduct. While in coppicing, a tree is felled close to ground level, so that straight stems then shoot up from the stump, to be used as poles within a few years, in pollarding, the original tree is cut about 9ft above ground level, to yield similar results.

We talk of the 'stone', 'bronze' and 'iron' ages, but all these 'ages', as well as those which followed until very recent times, were based economically on wood and wood products. Wood was of huge and vital economic importance: that is easy to forget, in our urban world surrounded by concrete, glass and steel. Houses, for example, were built around wooden frames. Lacking the long, straight, fairly thick poles which conifers produce, British builders could not construct log cabins, and instead devised the timber-frame house. Large hardwood timbers were shaped to make the frame, and the spaces were filled with whatever material was available – stone, or mud bound by thin sticks or straws to make daub-and-wattle. Such buildings were not necessarily primitive or ephemeral; substantial houses were built in this way, and some are still occupied, centuries later.

All the same, the introduction of iron had a devastating effect. By about 500BC agriculture was established locally, on the lighter and easier land, but although some places supported quite large human settlements, these were widely scattered. Most of the original forest remained untouched. The production and use of iron changed all that. Iron tools, much more efficient than any earlier ones, made forest clearance easier and led to advances in agriculture. The production of iron itself became a major industry, which required fuel for smelting.

When the Romans arrived, in AD40, they set to work to develop Britain and incorporate it into the greatest commercial empire in the world. Roman Britain was not a place of small isolated settlements, and bands of soldiers holding down a scattered and rebellious population; it became fairly densely populated, with many towns, and a countryside with some large villas and farms that were big even by today's standard. Though we like to imagine our ancestors fighting a kind of guerrilla resistance against foreign occupation, it was not really like that. It never is; people prefer to keep out of trouble and get on with the day-to-day business of living. Not far from my home in Cornwall, for example, the remains of a Roman fort were found. It was interesting, because Cornwall was never occupied by the Romans, although they visited it frequently in the course of their trade in metals. The fort was abandoned after about twenty-five years – a remarkably short lifetime for such a structure. The reason was apparently the docility of the people and the willingness of their leaders to collaborate with the imperial authorities. There was nothing for the soldiers to do, so they were posted elsewhere.

The prosperity brought by the boom in the iron industry had led to a population increase, with a consequent need for more farm land, and during the Roman period almost every corner of the original forest was entered. Agriculture could be confined to the best land no longer. By the time the Romans left and the Saxons arrived, something like half the original forest had disappeared from lowland Britain, and the clearance of the upland forests was proceeding, though more slowly.

The Romans, too, had many uses for wood, as they made Britain into one of the most important industrial and agricultural exporting regions of their empire. Fuel for the iron industry came mainly from coppiced woodland, and much iron was needed: the British industry supplied the Roman army, and British timber was used to build the ships for a provincial navy. The annual production of iron for Roman use was about 560 tons, and Oliver Rackham has calculated (*Ancient Woodland*, p108) that smelting would have consumed about 47,000 tons of wood, from about 36 square miles of coppiced woodland. It sounds little enough, but the industry must have been labour-intensive, and more land would have been needed to supply food and fuel for the workers, their families and the Roman garrisons under whom they worked. Nor was it only iron smelting and working for which the Romans needed fuel. They built with brick, and brick must be kilned. Their homes had central-heating and hot-water systems. They dried grain before storing it, just as farmers do today. They may have enclosed areas of woodland with earth banks, perhaps devising woodland management systems that continued after they themselves had gone.

The development sounds intensive, but the scale of Roman Britain can easily be exaggerated. At its peak the population did not exceed between half a million and 1.5 million.

The Saxons inherited a landscape that had been formed by the British and the Romans – including, of course, the trees the Romans had introduced – the damson and sweet chestnut, and the walnut which had ritual importance, because its seed is joined in two halves, so symbolising the union of marriage. There is no reason to believe the Saxons brought trees with them when they sailed to Britain, but they may have increased the growing of willow, possibly introducing white willow, and they may have introduced some hybrid elms. Certainly they made good use of the trees they found, and they gave us most of our common tree names. They made their spears from ash, a tree they also knew as 'axe', and like the Romans before them they made their shields from lime. Without returning to Saxon, you can trace the link in the similarity of modern English and German names: ash, *esche*; oak, *eiche*; birch, *birke*; beech, *buche*; linden, *linde*; elm, *ulme*.

When the Normans arrived in the eleventh century, almost the whole of Britain was settled. Where settlements were more than about four miles apart it was because they were in mountainous, moorland or wet areas – never because the forest resisted penetration. Nowhere could you travel in a straight line for more than about five miles through the forest without finding a village or hamlet, and many villages were several miles from the nearest woodland. It was rare to find a wood as much as 8 miles across, and even woods 6 miles across were uncommon.

The Domesday Book records that nearly half the settlements investigated had no woodland at all, and the relatively well-wooded areas were in the south-east of England, though not on the Downs which were open, and in patches in the east, north-west and west of the country. The largest wood at that time seems to have been on what is now Cannock Chase, covering 24,000 acres. The Domesday survey did not examine the whole of Britain: Scotland and most of Wales were excluded. However, it seems reasonable to extrapolate from the large area surveyed and to conclude that by 1086 the original primeval forest, the wildwood, to all intents and purposes had disappeared. England was not a dense forest with clearings; it was open farm land with woods.

Oliver Rackham, who made the calculations needed to translate Norman units of measurement into modern ones, and who concluded that the traditional picture of Domesday England was grotesquely wrong, was so startled by his own discovery that he examined it from many different points of view. He considered the number of ploughs that Domesday recorded, for example, to arrive at an estimate for the area of arable land, and found it occupied about one-third of England. He took the number of cattle and calculated the pasturage they would need, together with sheep and horses; he allowed for towns, gardens, and meadows. He found that the decline in woodland recorded in Domesday is if anything an under-estimate rather than an exaggeration.

What did Britain look like at that time? The total population was much smaller than it is today, of course, but today most of us live in large towns and cities. In Norman times the cities were small, most people living in villages or hamlets; and because crop yields were much lower several times today's land area was needed to feed each

Open farm land with woods

person. A journey across the countryside as it was then, avoiding all large towns, would give the impression of a land populated about as densely as it is now. Most of the villages of England existed then; indeed, some have disappeared since Domesday was compiled. Large areas would have been open, more or less treeless, and cultivated to grow wheat, barley, oats or rye. Woodland would have contained much more high forest in which most of the trees were fully grown, reminiscent of the wildwood, than most woodlands do today. The kind of plantation forest with which we are now familiar came much later. There would have been few conifers, and certainly no great tracts of coniferous monoculture, with trees growing in sharp-edged rectangular blocks up the hillsides. Nor was there much more forest then than there is now. By 1086 only about one-sixth of Britain was wooded, and probably this proportion had remained constant for several centuries before the Norman conquest.

Specifically woodland animals had been reduced in number, or were extinct. The brown bear was rare, possibly extinct, in Britain before the tenth century; those used for bear-baiting in medieval times were imported. The wild boar survived until the seventeenth century, but the beaver survived only in Wales and Scotland, and then only until the thirteenth century.

The clearance went on in the centuries which followed, as agriculture continued to expand into newly won land. It slowed during periods of famine or plague, but then resumed, remorse-lessly, so that by 1350 only one-tenth of the country was wooded. Rackham calculates that for two and a half centuries woodland was cleared at a rate of 17.5 acres a day; in the Weald of Kent some 450,000 acres were cleared. As the Middle Ages gave way to the

95

The chalk downs were among the first areas to be cleared of their original forest cover and since then they have been kept open by grazing. Sheep and rabbits destroy most tree seedlings, but outbreaks of myxomatosis which depleted the rabbit population, and declines in sheep farming, have allowed a few juniper shrubs to establish themselves. The wood in the background is very mixed, containing yew, beech, whitebeam, hawthorn and several other species *(M. Nimmo/Frank Lane Agency)*

Tudor period, the destruction continued. Now timber was needed to build the Royal Navy, whose importance was increasing rapidly, and the growing demand for iron was matched by the demand for charcoal. Charcoal, made by heating wood in the absence of air, concentrates the fuel, but consumes much wood in the process. In 1565 the woods of Furness were protected temporarily by a ban on smelting, but the ban was lifted about a century later, and eventually the industry had to move to Scotland because its fuel supply was exhausted. The increasing use of brick for building also made demands on the forests, sometimes large ones: following the Great Fire of 1666, London was rebuilt – in brick.

This phase in the clearance needs to be seen in perspective. It was less drastic than it may seem. When we think of the building of cities or navies, or of iron and steel production, we tend to think as people of our own century, measuring the population of a city in millions, the ships of a navy in hundreds. The ships of the Tudor navy were built from British timber, but by modern standards the ships were small and few. The use of wood to fuel the production of iron did not continue into the Industrial Revolution. Before that time the total output of iron was small and when it began to increase, as the Revolution began, water power was used; when that proved insufficient and gave way to steam power, the factories turned to coal as their principal fuel. Coal is a much better fuel than wood: it burns hotter and yields much more energy per ton consumed. Wood declined in industrial importance.

Yet there was some depletion of the nation's woodlands and it did not go unchallenged. Landowners were beginning to keep records of their holdings and the use to which their land was put, at least from the middle of the thirteenth century. The land was their capital and its produce provided their income; they knew that those who are profligate with their capital must come to penury. The earliest of those records describe a system of land use in which nothing was wasted. So far as woodland was concerned, the principle was simple: if a tree was felled, another must grow in its place. Often the anticipated annual yield from the woodland was stated explicitly. Rackham (*Trees and Woodland in the British Landscape*) quotes a management plan for Hayley Wood, West Cambridgeshire, dated 1356.

> A certain Wood called Heylewode which contains 80 acres by estimate. Of the underwood of which there can be sold every year, without causing waste or destruction, 11 acres of underwood which are worth 55s at 5s an acre. . . . A certain other Wood called Litlelond which contains 26 acres by estimate. Whose underwood can be sold as a whole every seventh year.

Eventually attempts were made to regulate the management of woodland by a series of statutes starting in the late fifteenth century; but they were intended mainly to formalise existing practice, conserving a tradition and preventing change, rather than being innovative. The 1543 statute, for example, requires that woods shall contain at least 12 standard trees per acre; that after felling woods shall be fenced so they cannot become wood-pasture; that woods must not be grubbed out completely. There were statutory penalties for infringements. That these were not enforceable was not really important; the statutes existed, and if leases were to be legally valid they had to acknowledge them in their terms. Whether the laws were regularly enforced or not, they were not ignored. Underwood used to be sold annually at woodsales, and it was sold standing – still growing – so that only the wood which was bought was cut. Records of some of those sales have survived and they include conditions of sale which refer to the statutory obligations.

The change from straightforward clearance to the maintenance of what today we call a 'renewable resource', which began so many centuries ago, was based upon a radical alteration in outlook. It was, if you like, a philosophical change that came to be reflected in legislation and practice, rather than some 'good idea' imposed from above. Perhaps it arose as attention shifted from the products, the materials that were actually used, to the land which was the source of those products. If so it was a consequence, possibly an inevitable consequence, of the adoption of a settled way of life.

If you are somewhat nomadic, moving your home every year or every few years, and if the food you need, and the raw materials to build your shelter and make your tools and equipment, lie around you, there for the taking, you will take them. If the materials consist mainly of wood, and if you need land on which to grow crops until the time comes to move, then you will clear the trees, using the wood you need and destroying the rest. If you are settled, on the other hand, a limited area of land has to go on satisfying your needs, perhaps for the whole of your life and that of your children and their children. So instead of thinking only of the materials themselves, and the ease with which they may be obtained, you begin to think about the land which produces them. It is from this altered perspective that the idea of land management may be born.

'Woodland', therefore, came to mean the land on which trees grew, rather than the trees which grew on a particular area of land. The next step followed from it, as people realised that they could remove some of the trees from woodland, or some of the underwood, and the woodland remained. Do it right, take only certain trees and try not to damage others as you do so, then allow the natural regeneration of young trees to compensate for those you have felled, and the woodland will continue to supply your needs for ever. Once that outlook was accepted it remained to devise detailed ways of optimising woodland management, of solving the list of discrete, practical problems.

Allow that the term 'woodland' refers to the land rather than to the trees, and all else follows, including a paradox. There are historical records of timber shortages from time to time. If woodland was being managed for sustained production, how did that happen? The answers, for more than one may be relevant, are simple. Remove too many fully grown trees in a short period, and until others grow to replace them there may be a shortage of timber. Yet the area of woodland remains the same, and probably the total number of trees remains the same. Alternatively, the shortage may be purely economic; owners of suitable trees may be unwilling to sell them for the prices offered. That, too, can create a shortage if the buyer refuses to offer more.

In 1664 John Evelyn's *Sylva* extolled the virtues of planting trees. Evelyn was not proposing forestry as we understand that term today, so much as a continuation of medieval practices by other means. The plantations were intended mainly for coppice. The Middle Ages saw the start of organised systems of woodland management, of measures to conserve woodland that began with ancient woodcrafts and absorbed them into a coherent structure. The wildwood was gone, and though possibly more wooded than it is today, Britain was a place of open landscapes. Yet the British had learned that if woodland was not to be lost completely, what remained had to be managed sensibly. It had to be conserved, and where possible its area had to be extended through new planting. The history of the human impact on the primeval forest thus has two parts. In the first, most of the forest was cleared. In the second the remaining woodland was conserved.

The modern history of British woodlands, from the Middle Ages to the present day, is dominated by the concepts of conservation and management. Yet that has not proved to be enough.

According to a three-year census compiled by the Forestry Commission to give figures for the total area of woodland in blocks of 0.25 hectares or larger, in 1980 in England 7.3 per cent of the land area was woodland, a figure that had increased from 6.2 per cent at the time of the previous census in 1947. In Wales 11.6 per cent was woodland, compared with 6.8 per cent in 1947. In Scotland, however, the total area of woodland had decreased slightly. In England broadleaved species accounted for about 57 per cent of the total woodland area, and in Wales for 30 per cent. Oak was the most common species in broadleaved high forest – woodland in which the quality of the trees and the density of stocking are such that the area can be managed sustainably on long rotations for the production of mature timber – but there had been a considerable reduction in the total area of oak woodland, especially in south-eastern England. Sycamore, ash and birch had colonised many areas at the expense of oak. The proportion of broadleaved high forest had increased from 34 per cent in 1947 to 45 per cent, due mainly to the abandonment of coppicing, so that trees had grown on to form a closed canopy, and what used to be areas of scrub had partly been planted and partly colonised naturally, so they, too, developed into high forest. Coppicing is becoming popular again, however, especially in the south.

The increase in the area of woodland sounds encouraging, but it has been due almost entirely to the planting of conifers, especially in the uplands. Conifer high-forest plantations now account for 47 per cent of the total high forest in England, and 74 per cent in Wales. They consist principally of Scots pine, Sitka spruce and Norway spruce, in that order.

The figures are vague about the age of woodland. One-third of the broadleaved high forest in England and one-quarter of that in Wales is more than 80 years old, but broadleaved high forest takes a long time to develop, so the statement is almost tautologous. The fact is that ancient and medieval woodland has been disappearing, and no amount of planting can replace it.

Ancient woodland grows on land that is known to have been wooded since before about 1600 and that consists of both primary and secondary growth. Primary woodland grows on sites that are known to have been wooded continuously throughout history, and secondary woodland is planted or naturally occurring woodland on sites that have not always been wooded. Basically, the older the woodland the better the habitat it offers to wildlife, and the greater the diversity of species that will usually be found in it. The implication for wildlife conservation is obvious. Ancient or medieval woodland is more valuable than recent woodland and primary is more valuable than secondary. In comparison, modern plantation woodland is inferior.

6
Management

The modern history of British woodlands is not simply a story of the restoration of timber lost many centuries earlier, but the conservationist element is strong. Those today who would preserve particular areas of woodland, who would reintroduce traditional systems of woodland management, and who urge us to plant more trees, especially more native trees, are not expressing a new view. They belong to a tradition, possibly a peculiarly British tradition, whose origins can be traced at least to the early twelfth century; and the idea may not have been new even then. Far from being despoilers of the countryside and indifferent to trees, the British love trees, often regret their loss, and would welcome more woodland.

In the Middle Ages, many villages had no access to woodland, yet they depended on wood as much as anyone else. Thus wood was traded – bought and sold and carried for long distances – so it acquired an economic value. When something has an economic value there is a clear incentive to manage it in ways that will enhance, or at least preserve, that value. Management was patchy, to be sure; not every landowner was a paragon. Yet at its best woodland management could achieve a regular yield that was sustainable indefinitely. It could do more. Before the invention of banking, a wood provided a convenient store for capital. It was not easy to steal, and as the quality of the product was not harmed by being cut a little early or late, it could be left standing when prices were low and cut when they improved. Because the plants are perennial rather than annual, the economics of woodlands are much more flexible than those of farms.

A clear distinction was made between woodlands producing wood or timber on a commercial basis, and wood-pasture, a more open kind of landscape in which livestock was grazed. The woodlands proper were permanent features of the landscape, and were protected; usually they were fenced, or surrounded by a ditch and bank, to keep out farm animals which would have damaged the young growth. Once trees are tall enough for their foliage to grow beyond the reach of browsing livestock, however, farm animals do no harm, and they would be admitted, so that in addition to growing trees woodland could help in feeding livestock. Much of the woodland was coppiced, in a cycle, so animals had to be excluded only from areas that had been cut recently, not from the whole of the wooded area. Farming and woodland management were integrated, two aspects of the same operation. In modern times we have separated those operations, and many conservationists and people who care for the aesthetic quality of our landscapes feel the separation has been too drastic. We should integrate them again so far as we can.

The terms 'wood' and 'timber' are not synonymous. 'Wood' consists of small poles, usually produced by coppicing or pollarding. 'Timber' is harvested in much larger pieces, as the trunks and largest boughs of fully grown 'standard' trees. It is possible to have a shortage of timber and a glut of wood at the same time. Indeed this situation has occurred more than once, and has led to some confusion among those who have studied the records and equated a shortage of timber with a decline in the overall woodland area, assuming the shortage to be due to excessive clear-felling without replacement or re-generation.

Many trees were pollarded. As we have seen, a pollard is a tree whose main stem has been cut about 9ft above ground level, removing all of the branches and upper trunk. New growth springs from the top of the severed trunk, and these small branches may be harvested at intervals for wood. Because their crop grows well beyond the reach of grazing animals, pollards thrive on land from which livestock is not excluded at all, and they were a feature of wood-pasture. Because they are taller, pollarded trees were used as markers. Often the trees on banks and in hedges would be pollarded, and those which could serve to mark off the woodland itself into discrete areas. Within woodland, most trees were coppiced and the

Pollarding involves cutting trees above ground level, usually at a height of about 9ft. As with coppicing, this encourages the tree to produce many new shoots from the stump, but the shoots have more protection than coppice shoots from the attentions of animals that enjoy eating tender young plants. These beech trees were pollarded long ago but their shoots were never harvested. The wood is at Selborne, the Hampshire village immortalised by Gilbert White (*M. Nimmo/Frank Lane Agency*)

If the demand is for small wood, coppicing or pollarding can produce it in abundance, as this pollarded oak illustrates. All these stems have grown from the stump left when the main trunk was severed (*M. Nimmo/Frank Lane Agency*)

most common management system produced 'coppice-with-standards' on a rotational basis.

Particular trees were chosen for use as large timber, being allowed to grow comparatively large before being felled, but their actual size varied widely. Builders were adept at using the timber supplied to them, sometimes without even removing the bark, and they could work with beams, joists and rafters that were not straight. If you have lived in an old house you will know that the right-angle is a distinctly modern invention! There was some need for very large timber, of course. The central shaft of a windmill had to be made from a single, huge tree-trunk. Large buildings needed large timber. Some trees, though, were considered to be of marketable size when no more than 6in in diameter; though many were larger than this when felled, most were not much larger, and were rarely as stout as a modern standard tree, though they may have been quite tall. An oak, for example – and oak was the tree that supplied most British timber – grows rapidly to its full height, then thickens more slowly. There were usually about a dozen such trees in each acre of woodland, and when one was felled a replacement had to be identified among the seedlings then establishing themselves. The remaining trees were coppiced, cut on a shorter rotation, almost to the ground. They regenerated as many small poles, and the small poles were harvested.

Since coppicing worked on a rotation, certain areas were cut each year, and the frequency with which particular trees could be cut varied. It was convenient, therefore, to have the coppice woodland divided into areas so everyone concerned could know from where the next crop must be taken – hence the marker boundaries were needed. Cutting was frequent, many areas being revisited every four to seven years. Seven years was the most common interval in medieval times, but the rotation was seldom regular; the system was flexible and responded to the demand for wood.

Pollarding and coppicing are two means to the same end. By the end of the fifteenth century, law required such conservative management of woodland, but by then it was general practice.

The ecological consequences of coppicing are profound if it is practised over long periods, and that is the main reason why its reintroduction is being advocated today. It is also part of the reason why conservationists prefer broadleaved to coniferous trees. If you cut down a conifer the stump and root die. If you cut down a broadleaved tree, usually new growth develops from the stump and the root does not die. At the same time, coppicing leads to great diversity of species.

105

The trees that are coppiced regenerate and go on regenerating for a very long time: far from injuring them, coppicing seems to extend their lifespans, so they become an almost perpetual source of wood. Chemically, the wood is composed of substances obtained from the air and soil, like any part of any plant, and cropping removes those substances. Livestock grazing among the trees returned some plant nutrient, but they, too, were removing vegetation by their grazing. The overall effect is a slow but steady export of plant nutrient and a decline in the fertility of the soil. This makes it sound as though the coppicing system is harmful, but harmful to what, or whom? Some plants are better than others at exploiting rich supplies of nutrient. Feed them well and they grow vigorously and, in relation to the plants around them, aggressively. On a fertile soil, therefore, the natural succession by which plants colonise an area will proceed fairly quickly to a situation in which a small number of aggressive species dominate the vegetation.

On a less fertile soil this cannot happen, because the aggressive species are denied the nutrients they need for vigorous growth. This allows the less vigorous species, with more modest requirements, to thrive. The final result is a great diversity of plant species. The ecological rule-of-thumb is that the greater the fertility of the soil, the fewer plant species will establish themselves on it; and if you prefer a great diversity of species you need a poor soil. Over the years coppicing produces poor soils, and so coppiced woodlands tend to have a rich diversity of plant species. The greater the diversity of plant species, the greater will be the diversity of animals feeding on them, and since the arrival of herbivorous animals is followed by the arrival of predators and parasites of those animals, the entire ecosystem is enriched.

The coppice-with-standards system left certain trees to grow to a much larger size. For management purposes the woodland was regarded as two distinct entities, underwood and fully grown trees, two sources of crops which were separated from one another vertically. This, too, was ecologically significant. The cutting of trees down to stumps removes the habitat of those species which live in the upper storey of woodland, among the tree-tops. Without standard trees, those species would have gone, but by retaining some standards the habitat was preserved. With or without standards, coppicing left untouched the bases of the trees and the ungrazed plants growing around them, so the general vegetation pattern suffered no major disturbance. This provided ample time, the other commodity that is required if an ecosystem is to develop fully.

106

Some high forest, managed for the production of timber and therefore not coppiced, still remained. It was not the kind of forest with which we are most familiar today. It had not been planted by humans, any more than the coppiced woodland had been planted. Individual trees might be put in to replace those that died or were felled, but this was a piecemeal operation; mostly the woodland was allowed to regenerate by itself, as mature trees reproduced naturally. The woodland was managed, of course, for the removal of materials from it, thinning seedlings that grew too close together, the clearance of underwood where this impeded pathways, all amounted to management. Yet the interference was minimal – with the trees, with the vegetation, and thus with the whole of the wildlife.

Nothing was wasted in coppice-with-standards woodland. Larger timber was used mainly for building. Smaller wood might be used to make furniture and other small items, and very small wood was used as fuel, along with inferior wood for which there was no better outlet. Even the tiny twigs, known in Devon as 'spray wood', were not thrown away: they were used to make charcoal and to fire bakers' ovens.

In the days before metal and concrete were used in building, more than 300 trees might be used to build a single farmhouse. Where

Woodland edge – a good habitat
for wildlife

larger timber was needed than most landowners could supply, the source was often the royal forests, where management was less intensive and standards grew larger. It was not until the sixteenth century that trees were grown to a much larger girth and cut into planks, and then on only a limited scale. Cutting planks was difficult when the work had to be done with hand tools. A saw-pit, rectangular and some 8ft deep – deep enough for a man to stand upright in it, far enough below the timber he was cutting to be able to work at it – had to be dug out with picks and shovels. This in itself was a big job. The pit could not be dug just anywhere: it had to be on ground high enough above the water-table for it not to fill with water. There are not many saw-pits left today, as many were filled in when the work was done, but some old sites may be found on higher ground. The tree-trunk had to be hauled to the pit and laid over it lengthways. It was cut by two men, one above, the other in the pit below, each holding one end of a long saw.

Planks are now cut by machines, but these arrived on the scene fairly recently. The first circular saw was being used in Holland in 1777, but it was later than that before all timber-yards had them.

The demand for planks did not change the traditional coppice-with-standards system. It meant only that some trees needed to be larger before they were felled. The general demand for larger timber, not just for making planks but for shipbuilding as well, influenced where standard trees were grown, for the obvious reason that the larger the tree the more difficult it is to move any distance. Large trees tended to be grown in greater numbers close to navigable waterways, and the closer they were to the shipyards the lower the transport cost and the greater the profit.

Coppice wood, too, was being cut when it had grown larger. The two developments were unconnected, but the growth of larger standards was accompanied by an increase in the length of the rotation. This varied widely, as said earlier, but in the Middle Ages it averaged about seven years, and by the end of the seventeenth century it had more than doubled, to about fifteen years. At the same time, the management became more systematic. Wood was no longer taken as the need for it arose, or when the price was right; it was cut at particular times, when it was ready, and the operation was planned over entire estates, not merely single woods.

At one time, when wood was the principal fuel, coppiced woodland supplied the local factories, the village baker, and all the surrounding community's heating and cooking needs. This sweet-chestnut coppice is in Kent (*M. Nimmo/Frank Lane Agency*)

Where woodland was lost altogether, almost invariably it was due to an extension of arable land. This remains the main cause of loss, and today it is accentuated by a decline in woodland management. The coppice-with-standards system has all but disappeared as the woodlands have lost much of their economic importance. But the disappearance is recent.

It is not true that the building of the Royal Navy, or of the British merchant fleet, in Elizabethan times depleted the country's stock of timber, far less of woodlands. As was mentioned in the last chapter, warships were small, and so were merchantmen. Although the fleets seemed impressive at the time, and they were of great political and economic importance, there were not very many ships in either of them. The climax in wooden shipbuilding came much later, in the early nineteenth century, but even that probably had little effect on stocks. It is true that the shipbuilders complained of a shortage of suitable timber, but their view was partial. There was plenty of timber. The trouble was that the paymasters in the Admiralty refused to give realistic market prices for the large timber they required, and they did not cast their net wide. They preferred to use timber supplied cheaply from the royal forests, and to augment it by buying from a small number of landowners who were their traditional suppliers. Britain got its navy cheaply, but the effect on woodlands was subtle. The demand from the shipbuilders increased the value of large timber, and so provided an incentive to conserve trees. When prices fell again, which they did and drastically, it did not pay to fell, and many trees grew to a very large size.

The ironmasters of the Industrial Revolution have also been blamed for destroying woodland, but that charge, too, may be unfounded. Wood was used to smelt iron, but most of it was in the form of charcoal made from coppice wood; small coppice twigs were cheaper than larger wood and did not have to be cut into small pieces before use. Nor was it long before the industry turned to using coal. Pumping engines, introduced at the beginning of the eighteenth century, allowed mine-workings to cut more deeply and more extensively into the measures, and by 1800 Britain was producing 10 million tons of coal a year.

That someone, or some industry or activity, had to be blamed for the apparent loss of trees reflects the British concern for trees and woodlands. Every tree is regarded as indispensible, every person who fells a tree is a vandal. Yet trees were indeed being lost. The eighteenth century, especially, saw the removal of many – but they were taken from hedgerows, wood-pasture and other places away from the managed woodlands. These were the most visible sites, of course, and though the effect of their removal may have been slight in relation to the national timber stock, it must have greatly changed the appearance of the landscape. It was due, as always, to the needs of agriculture.

The 'new husbandry' was being introduced to Britain from the continent, and farming was on the brink of becoming 'scientific'. Until then farmers had failed to resolve satisfactorily one of their basic problems: during the winter plants cease to grow, but herbivorous animals continue to eat. Hay made in summer can provide some winter feed, but it is never enough, and the slaughter of many animals before winter began had always been inevitable. Each spring started with herds and flocks reduced to a breeding nucleus, and a shortage of meat for consumers until newly born young could be raised to marketable weight.

The new husbandry introduced root crops to provide winter feed, and many more animals then survived the winter. At the same time it did away with the need to leave land fallow, by imposing a crop rotation to inhibit the build-up of weeds, pests and diseases specific to a particular crop, and by returning to the arable land a much increased quantity of manure from livestock. Until then manure had been returned to the land nearest the byres in which the animals spent the winter, but only as a means of disposal. The land receiving it grew better crops than untreated land further away, but no one knew about plant nutrients, and the fertilising effect of manure was not recognised until the middle of the nineteenth century.

The new husbandry revolutionised farming – and produced much of the enclosed landscape of the latter eighteenth and nineteenth centuries. It also made farmers much more prosperous and so encouraged them to make use of as much of their land as they could and to remove obstacles to cultivation, such as trees. The value of arable land increased, so more land was ploughed, and much wood-pasture was lost. Some woodland, too, was removed; although it did not amount to much, the overall visual effect must have been startling.

There was concern at the end of the eighteenth century that the increasing demand for coal by industry was raising its price, and so increasing the demand for fuelwood. This in turn was making small wood more valuable, and so discouraging landowners from producing timber. If the concern was well founded, any imbalance would have been temporary. With proper management the lifespan of a tree is more likely to be increased than shortened by cutting it, and when demand changed, timber production could have increased.

Trees were being lost, but they were also being planted. The eighteenth century was the age of ornamental plantations and semi-natural parks. It was also the period which saw the beginning of plantation forestry.

A deer seen in the wild in England is most likely to be a fallow deer (*Dama dama*). The adult deer stands about 3ft tall at the shoulder, has a fawn coat with conspicuous white spots and a black line down the back, and a tail which is black on the outside and white beneath, surrounded by an almost heart-shaped white rump patch. You might see a herd enjoying the sun in a field on a warm day, but they spend most of their time in woodland, especially in woodland with plenty of undergrowth, and often they wait until dusk to feed. Their story is interwoven inextricably with that of our woodlands.

They are not natives of Britain, but came originally from the Mediterranean region, the first of them brought over probably by the Romans, and more have been introduced since. They have been hunted for as long as there have been humans to hunt them, but up to the time of the Norman invasion they were not classed as game animals. The Normans changed that; they valued deer for food and for sport, and had no intention of allowing them to be delivered into Saxon cooking-pots. The deer were confined within large enclosures, where they could live an apparently free life but could be protected from predators, Saxon ones in particular. An enclosure for deer was called a 'park', and it contained trees because deer require trees. The descendants of those Norman herds are still living in Cannock Chase, Epping Forest and the New Forest. (Those in Epping Forest are predominantly black in colour, but they are fallow deer for all that.)

Other animals were kept in parks, including cattle and red deer, but the beast which is pursued across tapestries, in folk tales and in Hollywood historical romance is *Dama dama*. It escaped eventually, of course – like the rabbit, which was also introduced – and today fallow deer live wild in suitable places throughout most of the country. For a long time, though, it was a very serious offence under Norman law to take one without permission. The harshness of those laws is a recurring theme in British folk tales, and for once the stories are true.

The Normans in fact introduced a very radical change. Under Saxon law, hunting and access to the countryside in general was democratic. Anyone travelling through Saxon England, for example, who came across a person who had just killed a red-deer stag but had not yet skinned it, was entitled by law to a share of the kill equal to that of the hunter or of each of the hunters. The same applied to salmon, if someone arrived before the catch was shared among the fishermen. If a swarm of bees should arrive on your land, you must share it with anyone who asks you. If these laws sound strange to us now it is because we regard all land as being someone's private property, and the animals on that land as belonging to the landowner. That is the radically new idea brought here from France by the Normans.

No wonder people objected to it. Kill a game animal in the thirteenth century, and you would be fined. If you could not pay the fine you went to prison for a year and a day, and if at the end of that time you still could not pay, you were banished from England. If you lived inside a royal forest and owned a dog, three toes were amputated from each of its front feet so it could not hunt, and in 1390 Richard II assented eagerly to a petition that forbade anyone, anywhere, who did not own property from keeping any dog unless it was permanently on a leash or had its toes amputated. The penalty for breaking that law was imprisonment for one year.

The British park is not a recent invention, then, nor was it a very commendable one by modern standards of political morality. Indeed, if we accept the original definition – rather than assuming that a park must be a large garden well supplied with tarmac paths, swings and roundabouts – there were more of them in the Middle Ages than there are now. In the fourteenth century there may have been a park to about every 15 square miles over the country as a whole. Some were wholly wooded, a very few had no woodland, most were areas of grassland with scattered trees, most of which were pollarded. Britain's farming needed a lot of land, and large areas could not be spared exclusively for this form of livestock ranching; parks also accommodated cattle and sheep, even arable fields and common grazing. A park was defined as an area within which deer were confined and protected, but the land had other uses as well. In most cases the owner did not live in the park itself, or even close to it. He maintained a lodge for use when visiting.

Many of those medieval parks lasted for centuries, but their appearance changed with the use made of them. They were economic enterprises, farms of a kind, and in time the presence of the deer necessitated modifications. Fallow deer will feed on grasses quite happily, but they do have a liking for the young foliage of deciduous trees and shrubs, so can hinder the regeneration of woodland. Landowners had to make choices. They could fence areas of woodland against the deer and return them to conventional management, or they could abandon coppicing and crop only timber trees and some pollards, or they could get rid of the deer. The changes were made slowly, however, and when the age of the great landscape architects dawned in the eighteenth century they inherited the surviving medieval parks as the raw material with which to work.

Their modifications of the landscape were gentle and subtle. They could not engage in major earth-moving operations, for they lacked the machinery. They would remove trees here and there, plant here and there, alter or make a lake, and generally tailor a piece of countryside to make it fit the current notions of what was aesthetically pleasing. They were moulding nature according to an ideal. It was during this period that many ornamental stands of trees were planted.

Today those stands are close to the end of their lives, but they are of great visual importance to us. They were planted in the first place to produce a striking effect, and our taste in landscapes has changed little. We still find them attractive. Ecologically, however, they are of much less value. Wildlife requires continuity in space as well as time, with one area of habitat linked to other similar areas; the isolated oases provided by small ornamental copses are less congenial. Within woodland proper there are many sources of food, many places in which to find shelter, and sound woodland management is as likely to enhance the value of the woodland habitat as to injure it. The ornamental stands were designed for the enjoyment of humans; they were fairly open, and were kept open to provide pleasant walks. They are delightful to us, but they offer less food and less shelter to non-humans. More crucially, they are not linked by hedgerows along which small animals may move safely in their seasonal migrations in search of food and mates. A population in an ornamental stand is likely to be trapped, unable to cross the open ground, doomed to inbreeding and consequent genetic decline. This is not to say the old ornamental stands should be allowed to disappear. We may wish to replant them, to please ourselves, but we must see this as an addition to our main conservation effort, not as an important part of it.

The deliberate planting of woodland, as opposed to isolated trees, with a view to its commercial management did not begin until the sixteenth century and did not become important until quite recently. Most early plantations were intended for coppicing. Some were made to resemble older woods as closely as possible, by planting mixtures of seeds gathered from established woodland. (Seed was collected because, obviously, the removal of young trees would have depleted the woodland from which they came.) Others were intended to produce timber, and were planted with just one or two species thought suitable; often they were introduced species, and many were conifers.

Over the centuries, management altered the composition of British woodlands. Oak became more prominent; sweet chestnut established itself; more noticeably, elm invaded from hedgerows, increased, and so made good some of the losses of the ancient elm decline. By the later nineteenth century, however, the standard of woodland management had sunk very low; trees were not felled and coppicing had almost disappeared. Britain relied more heavily on metals and imported timber than at any time in the past. Henceforth, most British timber would be produced from commercial plantations and, as we shall see, these are quite different from the woods of former times.

Although they have fallen from commercial favour, woods produced by the old systems of management can still be seen, and as I have mentioned, those old systems are being revived. The woods listed below are arranged in alphabetical order of their counties. They are also listed in the Directory later in this book, which gives information on precise locations and points of access, and details of any permits needed before visiting.

Cambridgeshire Aversley Wood. A coppice-with-standards wood, with stands of pure hazel and mixed stands of hazel, ash and field maple. There are plans to reintroduce coppicing.
Devon Avon Valley Woods. Oak coppice woods, with some sweet-chestnut coppice. The area is not being managed as coppice, and some areas are being encouraged to develop into high forest.
Devon Buck's and Keivell's Woods. Oak coppice woodland, not being coppiced at present.
Devon Shaptor Wood. Part of the woodland comprises coppice-with-standards of hazel beneath a canopy of oak, which is being actively worked.
Dorset Fifehead Wood. A wood containing high forest and coppice-with-standards. The coppice, of hazel beneath a canopy of oak and ash, is being actively worked. The high forest is also being thinned.

(overleaf)
Aversley Wood, near Sawtry in Cambridgeshire, was traditionally managed as coppice-with-standards, and much of it has been woodland for thousands of years. It contains oak, ash, field maple and hazel, but also wild service trees, which are found only in ancient woodland. Aversley is also one of the largest woods in the county, covering 61 hectares (152 acres) (*The Woodland Trust*)

Dorset Horse Close Wood. A coppice-with-standards wood, of hazel beneath a canopy of oak. It is being actively worked.

Essex Stour Wood. A coppice-with-standards wood dominated by sweet chestnut. There are plans to reintroduce coppicing.

Gloucestershire Bigsweir Wood. Part of the wood contains coppice-with-standards of lime and beech beneath an oak canopy, where there are plans to reintroduce coppicing. The remainder of the wood is high forest, predominantly of oak.

Hereford and Worcester Pepper Wood. Coppice-with-standards of mixed species, actively worked by the local community, covers about half of the wood. Much of the remainder is managed high forest.

Kent Denge Wood. A coppice-with-standards wood, with sweet chestnut and hornbeam in separate areas; being actively worked. The wood also contains a fine stand of mature yew.

Kent Earley Wood. a coppice-with-standards wood, of mixed species, where active coppicing was reintroduced during the early 1970s.

Kent Park Wood. Coppice-with-standards of sweet chestnut and hazel in separate areas, which is being actively worked, covers about two-thirds of the wood.

Northamptonshire Stoke Wood. A coppice-with-standards wood of hazel beneath a canopy of oak and ash. This is one of the few woods in Northamptonshire where coppicing has been continuous, possibly for hundreds of years.

Surrey Chiphouse Wood. A coppice-with-standards wood of hazel beneath a canopy of oak and ash. Not being coppiced at present.

Sussex Brock Wood. A coppice-with-standards wood of hazel beneath an oak canopy. There are plans to reintroduce coppicing.

Sussex Guestling Wood. A coppice-with-standards wood of sweet chestnut, which is being actively worked.

Wiltshire Colerne Park. A coppice-with-standards wood, where until recently one of the main coppice species was wych-elm. This unfortunately has died, but the dead wood is being cleared and some regeneration is taking place from the coppice stools.

7
Forestry

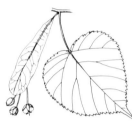

Forestry, as we understand it today, began some centuries ago. What is new is its scale and the general economic preference for plantations rather than permanent semi-natural woodland.

Throughout most of our history it never occurred to landowners, or seemed necessary, to plant large areas of land with trees of only one species, or at most a few, all the same age, to be felled at the same time to provide timber. Use of modern-style plantations was a response to trends and events that began at the end of the eighteenth century, accelerated in the nineteenth and early twentieth, and affected dramatically our use of land. Plantation forestry is 'modern' because not only is its rapid expansion a recent innovation, but the need for that expansion is a direct consequence of political and economic ideas that were tailored to the modern industrial and commercial world in which we still live.

The changes which led to modern forestry also changed farming. Indeed they came close to ending farming in Britain altogether, improbable though that may sound today – and anything that affects farming inevitably affects woodland. Although they have developed separately, and usually competed with one another for space, farming and woodland management are interwoven inextricably. They used to be closely integrated, when livestock grazed on land from which woodland products were taken. In the past farmers and owners of woodland often made use of the same land; they were often the same people. Our attempts to separate the two activities have not been entirely happy, but they are a consequence of the determined hunt for 'modernity'.

The story began with economic liberalism. During the nineteenth century, the British debated, and by the 1860s began to adopt, a policy of free trade with other countries. The liberal concept, with a philosophical and moral foundation which was the subject of fierce argument, evolved over many years from the British response to the ideas generated mainly in France during the Enlightenment. The eighteenth century had been a time of new ideas. The radical transformation of British farming began then, and commercial forestry was started in a few places in England and Scotland. If the *philosophes* of pre-revolutionary France had shown that our reason enables us to fit the phenomena of the universe into coherent patterns by which we may comprehend them, the industrialists of nineteenth-century Britain sought to impose patterns of their own. They believed, or behaved as though they believed, that the natural world could be made to supply human needs more abundantly than it had in the past. Wealth could be wrested from it, and if nature refused to be coaxed, it could be coerced. It was central to this belief that economies are governed by laws as absolute as those of nature, and that these laws must be allowed to regulate all economic activity. In effect, industry and commerce must be freed from all constraints imposed by governments, leaving the natural economic laws as the only regulator.

By the final quarter of the century, therefore, it was considered wrong, even immoral, to restrict imports by means of tariffs. Cheap food and other goods were imported from wherever in the world they could be obtained at the best price. But the effects on certain British industries were devastating. Agriculture and forestry were brought close to bankruptcy.

Britain became a net importer of food early in the nineteenth century. The Napoleonic wars curbed imports and caused huge price inflation at home, which temporarily enriched farmers, but when the wars ended and depression followed, attempts to protect British farmers, by means of the Corn Laws for example, were fought hard and eventually defeated. In North America, Australia and other parts of the world where land was plentiful and populations small, farming could afford to be less intensive than it was in Britain and therefore cheaper. The food surpluses it produced were huge, lowering prices still further, but the growers could make adequate incomes by selling in large amounts once they had found markets.

As British prices were forced down, so the value of land fell. Investment fell, too, for while farming was unprofitable, manufacturing industry offered good dividends and attracted capital. Farmers with a little woodland often had to clear and sell its produce just to raise the money to keep out the bailiffs. Probably this clearance had little long-term effect on the total area of woodland, because although it happened on a fairly large scale most of the farmers were too poor to remove the tree stumps and till the

120

cleared land, so the trees grew again. Britain was also importing timber, and that too was cheap. It came from the vast original, primeval forests of other countries. Such forests were not managed, far less planted, and the only costs incurred were those of felling and transport; even that was cheap, because logs could be floated for long distances down rivers, and sites for felling were chosen for their proximity to rivers.

By the early years of this century, therefore, both farming and woodland management were deeply depressed. Some economists even proposed that Britain should abandon agriculture entirely, rely on imports of food obtained more cheaply abroad than it could be produced at home, and direct all available investment into manufacturing, which was much more profitable. The occasional old-fashioned economist still advances this argument. It did not pay to farm, and it paid even less to grow trees. It seldom paid to fell them either, and so many woods grew on, neglected.

The German attempt to impose a submarine blockade of Britain in the 1914–18 war changed everything. It became painfully obvious that Britain could not continue to rely on imports for essential supplies that could be produced at home. Food prices rose, farming became profitable again, and large amounts of timber were taken from British woodlands. At the end of the war, in 1919, the Forestry Commission was formed, to build up a strategic timber reserve. Between the wars, however, depression returned, and farmers and woodland owners were plunged back into the miserable economic plight they had endured for so long. The respite brought by the war was ephemeral, and farmers were reduced once more to felling trees to pay debts.

British woodlands were also affected by disease. In 1908, oak mildew began to infect trees. It is a fungal disease which may make it more difficult for oaks to grow from seed, especially if the seedlings are shaded. Oaks provide food for a vast range of insects and can survive almost complete defoliation in spring, simply producing a fresh crop of leaves; occasionally, though, a severe and persistent attack can be too much even for them. Oliver Rackham reports that in 1916 an infestation of insects that had swept Europe reached Britain and continued for years, killing many trees. Dutch elm disease attacked in 1930, although not seriously.

The British strategic reserve was to be of timber, not wood. Demand had changed, and it was timber that was needed to make pit props, railway sleepers, telegraph poles and other large items; it was needed for the roofs of homes fit for heroes and of factories, and for cutting into planks to make floors. Large, straight pieces were wanted and they were to be provided by a comparatively new industry, forestry.

Forestry, the planting of trees for the purpose of timber production, does not aim to manage woodlands over protracted periods in order to produce a regular crop of small wood from the same trees. The method is to plant trees, grow them to timber size, fell them and replant – entirely different from traditional woodland management, with different requirements and objectives, and producing different results. Many people associate forestry, and the changes it brought, with conifer plantations, but the management change is no less if the plantations are of broadleaved trees. The important distinction is between permanent woodland and plantation, not between one kind of tree and another. In this sense permanent woodland is land on which trees are grown for a long period, during which there are always trees of all ages. Individual trees come and go, obviously, but no major change occurs in the character of the area.

The most obvious effect is on the landscape itself. A woodland that endures for centuries becomes an integral feature, always there because its management perpetuates it. The harvesting of coppice wood can be observed only within the wood itself, and even the felling of mature trees does not alter the general shape of the wood or its appearance. A plantation is very different. Land is ploughed and sown, and may remain rough and unsightly until the young trees become established. Then, as it grows, it comes to resemble something superficially like traditional woodland, but only superficially, because its trees are all of the same age and size. When fully grown it is clear-felled, and for a time disappears completely. This is tree farming, rather than woodland management.

Though the essential difference lies in the system of management, the trees themselves are usually different, too. If the aim is to produce marketable timber in the shortest time possible, then quick-growing conifers are much more useful than slow-growing broadleaved species. Long straight planks are what the customers want, so long straight logs must be grown, rather than the less

Trees that are being grown to their full size for timber should be broad, tall and straight. These magnificent beeches are growing in a plantation. For wildlife, the difference between a commercial plantation and more gently managed woodland is far more important than the difference between conifers and broadleaved species. In this plantation the trees are all much the same age and will be cleared together. A coppiced woodland, or one that is left fairly undisturbed, and contains trees of all ages from which particular trees are removed with as little disturbance as possible to the remainder, is richer in wildlife (*M. Nimmo/Frank Lane Agency*)

regular, often shorter, broadleaved trees. From the start of modern forestry, conifers have been the main crop.

This has had subtler effects than the changes to the landscape which we notice: the ecological ones. These begin with the soil itself. The leaves of broadleaved trees are decomposed more readily than the needles shed by conifers, because their cells contain more nitrogen in proportion to carbon. The decomposition of organic matter is based on the oxidation of carbon, which is converted into carbon dioxide. The nitrogen feeds the soil organisms concerned with decomposition. They use it to manufacture the proteins from which their own cells are made, and within those cells they use the carbon to provide them with energy – just as we do – by 'burning' it in the oxygen they respire. A change in the carbon : nitrogen balance which increases the proportion of carbon reduces the proportion of nitrogen; and the effect of a shortage of nitrogen is to suppress the population of micro-organisms in the soil of coniferous woodland, and to allow undecomposed needles to accumulate. The soil beneath the needles may be depleted of organic matter, which is being returned to it more slowly, and over many years its structure may deteriorate.

A deciduous forest is likely to support a wider variety of herbaceous plants than an evergreen forest. Few plants can tolerate dense shade well, and in a deciduous forest the fall of leaves each autumn opens the canopy. Sunlight can reach the ground, and before the spring growth of new leaves on the trees there is an interval during which plants adapted to woodland conditions can complete the vegetative part of their life-cycles: they can emerge, flower and set seed, and then can afford to disappear as the trees shade them once more. Most of the spring flowers that we prize so highly are woodland species which have evolved to live in this way. An evergreen forest affords them no such opportunity, for the shade is permanent as long as the trees stand.

Most animals are much less specialised in their feeding than some people suppose, but they do require some variety, and they need food they can reach. Spring flowers attract pollinating insects, such as bees and butterflies. The plants' leaves and seeds supply food for small mammals and birds, which in turn provide food for predators. The leaf litter on the floor of a broadleaved forest provides shelter and bedding material, and food for those organisms, including some of our most interesting fungi, which live on dead organic matter.

This is not to say that coniferous forests contain the planted trees and nothing else; some animals, such as the red squirrel, prefer coniferous forests. It is simply that in most of Britain coniferous plantations support fewer species than undisturbed or well-managed broadleaved woodland. The ecology of woodlands is discussed in the next chapter, but it is important here to look at the ecological difference between a deciduous and an evergreen wood, and the much more profound difference between permanent woodland and plantation.

That difference is threefold. In the first place it is due to the fact that when trees are planted commercially, only a limited number of species are used, and many or sometimes all of these are exotic. Because there are fewer tree species than would occur in a similar area of permanent woodland, fewer herbs and animals can find the food, shelter and other resources they need. The entire area is poorer ecologically than if it had developed naturally. Because so many of the trees are exotic, and not even naturalised, they satisfy fewer needs among the indigenous flora and fauna: fewer species can live on or near to them. Again, this makes the plantation ecologically poorer than permanent woodland.

The most important difference, though, is a consequence of the temporary nature of the plantation. A plantation may last for many years, of course, before it is felled. During that time the small animals which colonise the habitat may pass through fifty generations or more, so that from their point of view the habitat must appear stable. Yet it is not. It takes time for the small plants and animals within a community to arrive and become established, and for the community to grow dense and diverse. A plantation may last long enough for a community to form, but when the trees are cleared the devastation is total: everything goes and the habitat is destroyed. It will be replanted, but then the entire process must begin all over again. The shorter the rotation period, the poorer will be the community which shares the land with the trees, and it can never be as rich as that which develops in an area whose management extends over centuries and involves no abrupt, drastic alterations. You might find a very rare species in managed woodland; it is much less likely to live in or visit a plantation.

The most frequent criticism of commercial forestry plantations is that they intrude on the landscape, imposing dark green, rectangular blocks of trees that march across hillsides and dominate skylines. In recent years the Forestry Commission has become sensitive to this criticism and provided the Commission continues to manage the national forests we are less likely to see such ugly planting in future. That it happened in the past is a result of British land-use policy. While afforestation was necessary if we were to become less dependent on imports for our timber supplies, it was felt

that forests must not interfere with farms. Land which could be farmed should be farmed, and trees should be grown on land which had little agricultural value. Consequently, the Forestry Commission bought land in the lowest of the grades which are used, somewhat crudely, to classify the productive value of farm land. Much of this is in the uplands, on the higher slopes, on the tops of hills and on moors.

Trees, even coniferous trees, are just plants. They require conditions not much different from those needed to grow plants of any other kind. Indeed, Britain lies close to the geographical limit for most broadleaved trees, many of which have modified their reproductive behaviour in response to the harsh conditions offered them here. At one time they grew on the land now occupied by farms. It was the expansion of farming which displaced them and it seems inappropriate to require them to occupy a larger area, but only on condition they do not trespass on to the land that formerly was theirs. The best place for woodland, so far as the trees themselves are concerned, is on farm land. Land which is marginal for agriculture is no less marginal for forestry.

The problem was solved, up to a point, and the use of conifers helped because they are more tolerant of poor conditions. On harsh sites trees can be established if they are planted close together in blocks, to shelter one another. The edges of the blocks must be regular because an irregular edge would expose some individuals to cold, drying winds; they would die, and the intended irregularities would be smoothed away – by the weather. But such harsh sites are on high ground and therefore visible from afar. The Forestry Commission has been blamed for a style of planting which, to a large extent, was imposed upon it.

If plantations are to sit more gracefully in the countryside, and are to blend with farms, then they must be located on lower ground, perhaps on farms but certainly adjacent to them. Agriculture and forestry must be integrated once more, rather than being placed in artificial opposition to one another.

Commercial conifer plantations can be very intrusive where rigidly rectangular blocks are laid like a huge, grotesque patchwork across the rolling grandeur of an open hillside. The patches, each containing trees at a different stage of development and therefore of different colours and textures, are bounded by access paths and roads, with two main areas divided by a public road that was almost invisible before the dark green of the forest highlighted it. Most newer plantations have been imposed on landscapes with a little more sensitivity than this – an example of forestry at its worst (*M. Nimmo/Frank Lane Agency*)

This need not require the abandonment of any policy objectives. On better land forests would produce higher yields, so a smaller area would be needed for each ton of product. Because weather conditions would be more benign, the blocks could be smaller, with irregular edges that blended through belts of broadleaved species and into surrounding land. A quite modest intensification of the farming system could compensate for lost agricultural yields from the land used, if this were considered necessary. A further benefit would be that smaller, more complex and more productive plantations would require more intensive management and so would provide more employment in rural areas.

It is widely accepted today that the sharp distinction drawn between farming and forestry was a mistake, and led to distortion. The Forestry Commission's recent sensitivity to environmental criticisms is based partly on economics. Its own economists calculated the return it could expect on its capital investment as between 1 and 3 per cent each year. Since this has been lower than the annual rate of inflation for many years, the difference between the two has been amounting to a notional public subsidy of an unprofitable enterprise. It was felt, therefore, that the Commission needed a justification for its operations beyond the production of timber. So it began to place considerable emphasis on the employment it provides in rural areas that were losing population. It pointed out that while it is expensive to create new jobs in forestry, afforestation can provide twice as many jobs as agriculture in a given area. Forests have been opened to the public and the Commission now welcomes the visitors and provides excellent facilities for them. Throughout Great Britain there are almost 600 picnic sites and around 600 forest walks and nature trails on Commission land, as well as nearly 200 holiday houses and cabins.

The Forestry Commission does not operate only in the uplands. It has acquired lowland woods as well, and its treatment of them has been dictated by the economics of its kind of forestry. If the lowland woods are unproductive, as they often are when compared to conifer plantations, they are cleared and when their replanting is planned the curious distinction between farm land and woodland reaches splendid heights of absurdity. If forests can be established only on poor land, therefore land which is wooded must be poor. Since it is poor, the most appropriate use for it is to convert it to commercial forestry plantation. Mixed woodlands, some of them perhaps centuries old, have been cleared and replaced by conifer plantations.

It is this process that has led to the loss of much of our remaining ancient woodland and although conservationists have protested, all too often they and the foresters have found themselves at cross-purposes. Their views of conservation differ. To the forester, the main task is the economic production of timber. This is not incompatible with allowing such herbs and animals to live in the plantation as may choose to do so. They may even be encouraged and protected so far as this does not interfere with the task in hand. So the forester may claim to be a conservationist. Other conservationists prefer to see an area as a complete system, a total community of plants and animals along with the non-living constituents of their environment. Communities are encouraged to thrive by establishing appropriate conditions for them and then leaving them more or less alone. Where there is management, and often there has to be some, its purpose is to improve the habitat.

The two views are irreconcilable, but compromise should be feasible: the economics of land-use must be made a little more flexible by allowing that the countryside serves purposes other than the production of food and raw materials – purposes that may be difficult to evaluate in purely financial terms. The conservationists would like to see woodlands of high ecological or historical value identified, and then managed in ways that preserve the features which give them their value. This does not necessarily mean a high wall must be built around them. Indeed, since most of them have been managed for most of their history and their present quality is largely a result of that system of management, its restoration is often the best way to preserve them.

The Forestry Commission may not be the body best suited to such a management system: the output of timber would be small, while the output of coppice wood, for which the Commission has no great market, would increase. Yet the Commission needs to earn money. How can it afford woodlands that are no more than a liability to it?

There are no easy answers, but it is possible to make hints. As suggested, the reintegration of woodland management with farming might ease the economic pressures a little, and would certainly produce more attractive landscapes. The Commission itself might increase its earnings by adding more value to some of the timber it produces already. Though its main task is to supply British industry with raw timber, it might go a stage further. In Cornwall, where I live, both the Duchy and the Commission own woodlands, and the Duchy woodlands are said to be by far the more profitable. This is because they do not sell only raw timber; they also sell products made from wood, and sell them on a large scale. Their sales are 'visible', because every article bears a little 'Duchy Woodlands' badge to identify it, and you find this everywhere on gates, fences, garden furniture, almost anything made from wood. The Duchy also sells young trees, from one of the best tree-nurseries in the area. That, too, must be a profitable undertaking, and it is a nursery, not a garden centre: it sells only plants.

In the end, though, we may need to decide priorities. If we need as much timber as the country can possibly produce, then how high a price are we willing to pay for it? Are we willing to sacrifice what remains of our most interesting, and ecologically and historically most valuable woodlands? If not, then we may have to provide adequate protection for these areas, pay for their maintenance, and if necessary allow timber imports to increase to compensate.

Today the Forestry Commission is one of the largest landowners in the country, controlling directly about 4,800 square miles, more than 5 per cent of the total land area of Great Britain. Not all of this is planted, but more than 3,500 square miles are, in a country with some 86,500 square miles of land area. The Commission is responsible for all the state forests, but its influence extends further: it issues the licences without which it is an offence to clear-fell private woodland, and it also licenses the thinning and felling of crop timber on private land. It can award grants for private afforestation, conducts its own research, and has much useful advice to offer.

It remains unpopular with conservationists. The view of the Woodland Trust is that although the Commission's stated objectives these days take much greater account of conservation and the environment, the theory does not always translate into practice. When decisions are made, which means at the local level where its officers meet landowners face to face, it may still advocate exotic plantations. Large organisations are composed of individuals, and individuals see things and interpret instructions and guidelines in different ways. In my experience, however, the advice given to private owners of woodland is often sensitive. In some cases the Commission has not encouraged the planting of solid blocks of trees, whether conifers or broadleaves, if there is an alternative. Its officers have seemed well aware of the disadvantages of plantations

When a block of trees has been felled and the ground is bare and devastated it is time to prepare for the next crop. Here, in Delamere Forest, near Northwich, Cheshire, a tractor is drawing a heavy rotavator. While this work is in progress the noise and disturbance will drive away all the vertebrate animals and the ground flora will be destroyed. It will recover, but only temporarily, because within a few years the new crop of trees will shade the ground, and then it will be time to fell them and replant (W. Broadhurst/Frank Lane Agency)

of any kind in which all the trees are of the same age. They have recommended programmes of planting spread over many years, with quick-growing conifers to provide a cash crop sown among the slower growing native broadleaved species.

My impression may be inaccurate, but it hardly matters because the trend in large-scale timber production is clear, and the owners of small private woods have little part to play in it. In years to come the pressure to increase the plantation area in Britain will grow. We still import 92 per cent of our timber, and Forestry Commission studies have suggested that of the 11,600 square miles of land which could be afforested, between 400 and 650 should be planted between now and 2025. The Centre for Agricultural Strategy of the University of Reading has proposed still more extensive plantation, of up to 1,700 square miles in the same period.

This new planting is likely to be more intensive and more highly commercial than forestry has been in the past. The forestry industry appears to be following the path of intensification which agriculture pursued in the 1950s and '60s. Investment will increase, more use will be made of machinery and fertilisers, crops will be induced to mature more rapidly, and the labour force will be reduced. There is no reason to suppose that the new forests will not consist mainly of conifers – and there are other grounds for supposing we may see more conifer plantations in future.

As long as so much British woodland remains under the direct control of the Forestry Commission, or under its strong influence, we can hope that its environmental sensitivity will persist and grow. The Commission, after all, has a statutory obligation to conserve wildlife and landscapes, and to serve the public. It can be reminded of this when the need arises. If the state forests are transferred to the ownership of corporations and city institutions, we can only hope that they inherit such awareness of conservation as the Commission has acquired. Of course there are private landowners whose management is exemplary: the 6th Earl of Bradford established woodlands on his estates that won the admiration of all who saw them and who care about sensitive woodland management; they survive to provide models for other landowners.

There are three ways to manage trees in order to yield wood which can be sold commercially.

Woodland may be integrated fully with grazing, to produce wood-pasture. This does not encourage very effective tree management, however, because trees in pasture, or in hedges, are widely spaced and are often grown to their full timber size, when they must be felled and replaced.

Traditional woodland management produces a sustainable yield that is known to continue over centuries and may be able to continue over millennia. It can be highly productive, but it is labour-intensive and can be justified only by a fairly high demand for small wood and wood products.

Commercial plantation forestry produces only timber, which is obtained by clear-felling, followed by replanting.

In modern times, while forestry has increased dramatically, traditional woodland management has declined almost to the point of disappearance, and wood-pastures have become rare. Yet it is this management which produced the woodlands so typical of the British landscapes and so valuable for wildlife. The change to forestry is a major one, and perhaps we should try to prevent it from proceeding further at least until we have had time to evaluate the real meaning of that change.

Meanwhile the Woodland Trust in particular, and all conservationists in general, believe that the loss of ancient woodland must be arrested now and arrested completely. Too much has gone already. We can afford to lose no more.

8
Woodland Life

A wood is much more than a collection of trees. It is a complete, complex, living community of plants, animals and micro-organisms. The trees are the most visible members of the community, and because of their size they exert great influence within it, but they do not have it to themselves, and they depend on many of the other woodland organisms for their own wellbeing.

There have been many surveys of woodland populations, but the simplest way to gain an impression of what they comprise is to compare the total mass of each group of organisms in a particular area. The total mass of organisms is known to ecologists as the 'biomass', and a self-contained, self-sustaining community of organisms is an 'ecosystem'.

In a typically British woodland ecosystem, dominated by oak and beech, each acre of land is likely to contain about 100 tons of woody plants – much of the weight being dead wood lying on the ground – half a ton of herbaceous plants, 1.5 tons of fungi, rather less than 2lb of large mammals such as deer, about 4.5lb of small mammals such as rodents, just over 1lb of birds, and half a ton of the larger soil animals, including more than 500lb of earthworms, 50lb of spiders, 9lb of beetles, and 90lb of slugs and snails. Apart from the soil animals, there are single-celled organisms, including nearly 4 tons of bacteria and about 340lb of protozoa.

Obviously the soil is the most densely populated part of the ecosystem, but its population is not distributed evenly. Soil organisms form a kind of patchwork pattern, the design of the patchwork being related to the location of the trees. In a deciduous forest, leaves may seem to fall everywhere, and lie evenly over the entire forest floor, but a close look shows that they lie more thickly in some places than in others; they drift, much as falling snow drifts. As you move away from a tree of one species toward one of another, the leaves not only look different but differ in their chemical composition. All the leaves are eaten and all but 1 per cent of them are eaten after they have fallen to the ground. The organisms which consume them crowd most densely where the food is most abundant, and each crowd of leaf-eaters includes many of those which have a preference for the leaves of the particular tree which contributed most to the leaf pile.

Dead wood is also eaten, but more slowly. It represents a large source of food, and is exploited by fungi, such as the familiar bracket fungi. The fungi in turn are eaten by beetles and flies. Very few multi-celled animals can digest wood directly, but fungi can, and the animals can digest fungi. A few insects, such as termites, can eat wood directly, but it is digested for them by colonies of bacteria living in their guts. The fungi, insects and other small animals and micro-organisms provide food for predators, and those predators are hunted by higher predators. Half of the birds which live in woodland feed on the ground, many of them on insects.

The trunk of a fallen tree may seem to disappear slowly, but in general dead material is removed at remarkable speed. If you consider the mass of leaves produced within an area of woodland in a single year, falling to the ground in autumn to swirl about your ankles and crunch beneath your feet on a fine day, the sheer volume is impressive. The leaves become wet and form a carpet, and you might expect them to accumulate, making that carpet thicker each year. They do not, because everything is eaten.

Almost all the food value in the leaves and wood is used to supply living organisms with energy. As mentioned in the last chapter, the food is 'burned', the carbon which comprises most of its bulk oxidised to carbon dioxide. Because the organisms which consume the dead material live in the soil, it is there that the carbon dioxide is produced. If you take an area of forest floor, the amount of carbon dioxide held in the soil below ground level is much more than the amount in the column of air above it from ground level to the top of the atmosphere. In tropical rainforest, where the turnover of material is large and rapid, the soil can contain thirty times more carbon dioxide than the air above it. This is why some scientists fear that the clearance of very large areas of forest around the world may affect climates, by releasing all of that carbon dioxide.

Trees themselves alter the climate around them. You can feel the change distinctly the moment you enter a wood. In summer it is cooler, and in winter warmer, than in the open, outside the wood, and the wind blows more gently. Usually it is wetter, and rarely is it drier. All the larger plants transpire water. Nutrients move through plants in solution, and it is water which 'fills' plant cells and makes

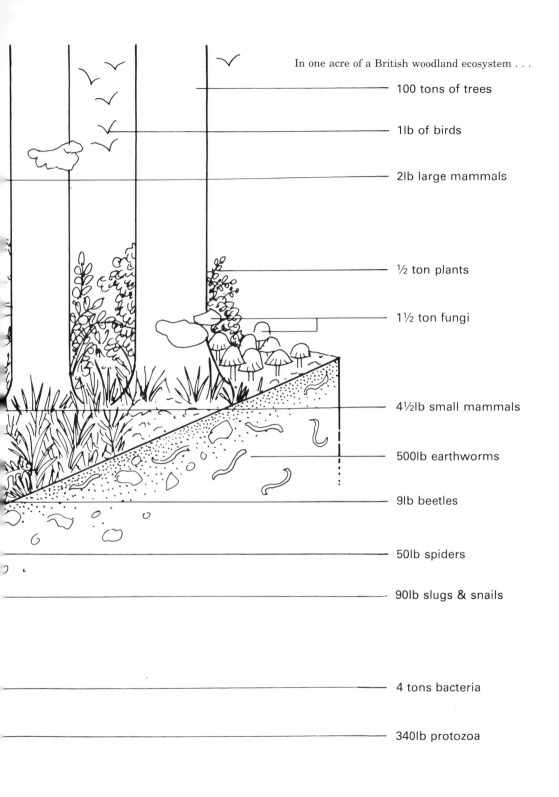

In one acre of a British woodland ecosystem . . .

100 tons of trees

1lb of birds

2lb large mammals

½ ton plants

1½ ton fungi

4½lb small mammals

500lb earthworms

9lb beetles

50lb spiders

90lb slugs & snails

4 tons bacteria

340lb protozoa

them rigid. If a soft-leaved plant, such as a lettuce, has insufficient water it collapses physically: its leaves will become limp. Give it water and in a short time its leaves will be firm once more. Water moves through plants because the pressure at the upper end of the system is much lower than the pressure at the bottom end. This pressure difference is due to the evaporation of water from the upper end, through the small pores in leaves called 'stomata'. The water evaporates, causing a reduction in pressure, which causes more water to be drawn from below, and so a flow is maintained. The water which evaporates enters the air, and that is why the air inside a wood is usually moister than the air outside the wood.

The climate is more equable in woodland because the trees provide shelter from the wind, and because they shade out much of the sunlight. You can tell how much sunlight they intercept by the pattern of herbs which grow near the ground. The trees themselves alter the chemistry and water balance in the soil and so to some extent select the plants which grow near their bases, but this influence wanes as the distance from them increases and there are few trees which suppress all other plants in their neighbourhood. If the shade is intense, so that less than 10 per cent of the sunlight reaches the ground, the ground will be bare. If there is a little more sunlight, mosses will grow, and if about one-quarter of the sunlight reaches the ground the mosses will grow abundantly, covering dead wood and much of the ground itself. If one-quarter to one-half of the sunlight reaches the ground, you will find grasses, and if still more light is available there may be heather and ling, whose presence indicates that the tree canopy is fairly open. An open canopy also favours the growth of smaller trees, where for part of each day they can receive direct sunlight.

It does not help, though, to visit a wood on a bright sunny day and look for the sunlit patches. The woodland floor receives much more light on cloudy days than on sunny days. The light is more diffuse when the sky is overcast, and it enters the wood from many angles. That is why there are fewer shadows – the light is distributed more evenly.

Trees also intercept rain and snow. On open ground precipitation falls evenly, but in woodland it does not. Rain runs along leaves and drips from them, and snow may be held on branches high above the ground. Just as we may shelter from the rain beneath a tree, so there may be an area around each woodland tree which is perpetually sheltered, and which receives its moisture through the soil laterally, rather than vertically.

Beneath the ground, the tree roots absorb mineral nutrients. The

The woodland cycle

leaf litter, the dead wood, the bodies of dead animals and droppings
of live ones, all the organic matter consumed by the organisms
which decompose material, are reduced to ever-simpler chemical
compounds, which eventually reach a form that can be used directly
by plants. They cycle from the soil back into plants, perhaps to
animals, back once more to the decomposer organisms, and so back
to the soil again. Some of them, such as carbon and nitrogen, enter
the air during part of their cycle, others enter water.

Plants depend on their root systems for their supply of soil
nutrients, and the root system is always large compared to the part
of the plant which is above ground. The roots do more than feed the
plant; they also anchor it, and a tree requires a substantial anchor.
The root system of a mature oak may weigh three times more than
the part of the tree growing above ground. A tree requires large
amounts of nutrient, and so the soil around it is likely to be poorer
than soil further away, and the acidity of the soil is likely to be

139

6

7

different. Oaks produce a very acid soil, but in general the soil acidity increases as you approach any tree, and the amount of plant nutrient available in the soil decreases.

A woodland ecosystem can be divided into layers, or strata, because it is much more three-dimensional than, say, grassland. In an old wood, supporting many kinds of plants and animals, you may find seven strata. The highest comprises the tallest trees: this is the main storey, and if you look at the woodland from a distance you will see that the canopy is all more or less at the same height. A few trees may grow above it, but it is difficult for them to do so, and most such attempts are checked. There is more sunlight above the canopy, so that a tree which was taller than its neighbours could photosynthesise more, but the wind is also stronger above the shelter of the tree-tops, and the tender growing shoots and leaves of a taller plant would be dried and chilled, and would wither.

In coppiced woodland, the coppiced trees form the main storey, and the woodland is much lower than if it was left to grow unchecked.

Below the main storey there are smaller trees – those more than 30ft tall, clearly trees rather than shrubs, but not reaching to the main canopy. They may include young individuals of the dominant species or smaller trees like hazel, hawthorn, rowan or holly, or in wetter areas willows perhaps. This is the understorey.

Guelder rose,
an understorey shrub

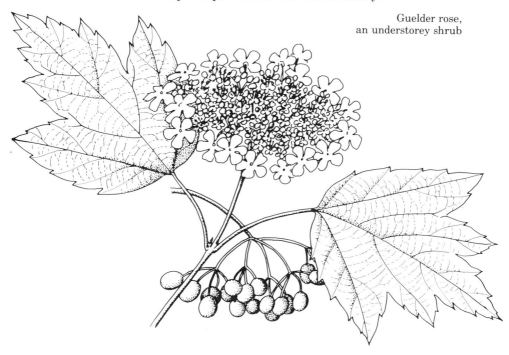

Solomon's seal (top) with lily-of-the-valley
– two well-loved woodland
perennials, now found all
too seldom

Still closer to the ground is the shrub layer, formed by woody plants between 3 and 30ft tall. Hazel and holly might occur as shrubs where they are too shaded to grow larger. Below that is a dwarf-shrub layer, of woody species less than 3ft high such as brambles. Heather and ling may form part of the dwarf-shrub layer in very open woodland.

The tall herb layer is composed of non-woody plants more than 3ft tall, such as nettles, on wet ground the extremely poisonous hemlock water-dropwort (*Oenanthe crocata* L.), or wall lettuce (*Mycelis muralis* (L.) Dum.). Below them are the smaller non-woody plants, the bluebells, daffodils, primroses, ferns and other low-growing and very beautiful plants which comprise the field or herb layer. Finally, there is the ground layer, the liverworts, mosses and similar plants which grow on the ground itself.

Each layer provides food and shelter for a population of animals, and sometimes of epiphytes – the plants such as creepers, lichens, mosses and some ferns which grow on other plants, but use them only for support rather than as a source of nutrient. Birds, especially, are distributed vertically through woodland because of their nesting preferences. One survey of oak woodland found that 15 per cent of birds nested on the ground, 31 per cent in or on tree-trunks, and 29 per cent in the foliage, but that half the birds fed on the ground.

Insects are to be found high in the upper storeys of a wood. Woodpeckers and tree-creepers are adept at chipping away bark and prising them from their lairs. Wood-eating beetles, wasps and sawflies which lay their eggs in wood, and even some flies, feed on the trees themselves.

Many of the insects and small mammals move between the ground and the upper storeys. Some of them spend the winter beneath the soil and climb the trees in spring. The most famous climbing mammal of the woodland is the squirrel. The red squirrel (*Sciurus vulgaris* L.) is a native inhabitant, most abundant in conifer plantations, preferring Scots pine but making do with other species. It will move into mixed woodland provided it contains plenty of conifers, or even into broadleaved woodland, especially of beech, when its own numbers rise and its habitat is crowded. Red squirrel numbers have fluctuated widely over the years. They disappeared from southern Scotland in the early eighteenth century and during the century after that they almost vanished from the Highlands, although they were reintroduced. Abundant from about 1860 to 1900, they then declined, by 1930 had increased again, and by the 1940s another decline began throughout Britain. Numbers

143

Bluebell

have now started to rise in parts of Scotland. The declines seem to have been due mainly to the destruction of their habitat. They may also have suffered from a disease epidemic, but this is not likely to have produced a serious lasting effect.

When the large conifer plantations were established earlier in this century the red squirrels were unable to colonise them, because the more versatile grey squirrels (*Sciurus carolinensis* Gmelin) had moved in ahead. Probably the reds would have returned more rapidly were it not for the grey squirrels, which occupied their old habitat. The grey squirrel prefers broadleaved woodland, but it will make do with conifers if it must.

The grey squirrel is a recent introduction: the first records of it in Britain date from the late 1820s, in North Wales. It came from North America, where it prefers to live in dense hardwood forests, but has become thoroughly naturalised here.

144

Both squirrels search for food throughout the woodland, but carry items right up in the tree canopy to eat. They have a varied diet, the grey squirrel preferring acorns to all other foods. Both of them strip the bark from trees and nip the growing points from trees they prefer, causing considerable damage and sometimes killing the trees. They will also take cereal and fruit crops from nearby farms and orchards. Most people find squirrels attractive, engaging animals, and because it is scarce the delightful little red squirrel is no threat at present and should be conserved. The grey squirrel, however, is a serious pest of woodland.

Locally, in Hertfordshire and Buckinghamshire only, the edible or fat dormouse (*Glis glis* L.) is a similar pest. It is about twice the size of the common dormouse, rather greyish in colour, and has a bushy tail, so you might easily mistake it for a small grey squirrel. It too is a recent introduction, stemming from an escape in 1902 from a zoo at Tring which Lord Rothschild used to keep.

Squirrels are among the 'Johnny Appleseeds' of the woodland: they plant tree seeds, as well as other food items, with much

Red squirrel

enthusiasm. In theory, of course, the hoards of buried seeds provide their owner with food during the winter; in practice it does not entirely work out. The squirrel probably remembers the general area where it stored food, but it relies on scent to locate the caches, and cannot smell them at all when the ground is dry. Despite their reputation for thrift, squirrels do not plan ahead. They bury food when there is more of it than they can eat at once, as a response to the surplus. But the adaptation is useful to them, especially in those parts of continental Europe where winters are much harsher than in Britain.

The dormouse, hazel dormouse, sleeper or dory mouse (*Muscardinus avellanarius anglicus* Barrett-Hamilton) is also an agile climber, but you will be lucky to see one. Squirrels feed by day and visit the ground often, dormice feed by night and spend most of their time in their nests, up to 15ft above ground – and they are tiny. They were thought to be very rare, but recent surveys suggest they are fairly common over southern England as far north as the Midlands. They like coppiced woodland, and prefer to feed on the seeds of hazel, sweet chestnut or beech.

The most typical woodland mammal is the wood mouse (*Apodemus sylvaticus* Hinton). It requires shelter, and is very nervous. It forages by night, but even a bright moon will keep it at home, although its principal enemy, the owl, hunts by hearing, not by sight, and darkness is no protection against the sharp talons borne on silent wings. The wood mouse lives on, or just beneath, the ground, where there is bramble or bracken, and it travels its range by paths it makes through the leaf litter. People sometimes worry about the fate of small woodland animals when the ground is buried deep beneath snow. In fact they fare very well. The snow lies on top of the vegetation, and they can move quite freely beneath it. Their winter food consists mainly of seeds, which are as likely to be found on the ground as anywhere else, and as they move and feed they are hidden from predators. For the rest of the year the wood mouse feeds on seeds, small seedlings, buds, fruit, insects and slugs.

It shares its habitat with the bank vole (*Clethrionomys glareolus* Schreber), which is common in all deciduous woodland that offers areas with thick cover. It is much more of a climber than the wood mouse, so much less dependent on what may fall from above; it climbs trees in search of soft fruits, seeds and leaves.

Both these small rodents have a well-developed social organisation. A bank vole forages over an area up to about half an acre, and may have many encounters with other voles; it distinguishes a member of its own local group from a stranger by scent, and it also communicates – by ultrasound. Males prefer to mate with females which are close relatives. Voles are not aggressive, but like other small rodents they will chatter angrily, and a dominant male will chase subordinates away from food.

A wood mouse lives in a range of about 5 acres. The range will have a dominant male, but subordinate males and females are permitted to feed in it, sometimes doing so in groups. Mice can be aggressive, and at certain times of year the dominant males bully their subordinates and the young. Females will fight to defend the areas in which they breed.

As with many small mammals, in addition to the resident mice there is a travelling population of individuals which are probably seeking areas in which to settle. During winter they remain wherever they happen to be, and are tolerated, but in spring, when the community becomes more active, they are driven away by the residents.

The small mammals attract predators. Badgers and foxes, both of them highly social animals living well-ordered lives, have their quarters in earth banks where the ground cover is dense. They eat considerable amounts of plant material, but they also eat mice and voles. Stoats and weasels hunt them too, and the owls are very dependent on them. More than two-thirds of the diet of the long-eared owl (*Asio otus*) consists of mice and voles, and so does up to half the diet of the tawny owl (*Strix aluco*).

Several bats roost and hunt in woodland, and together the bats consume vast numbers of flying insects. The noctule (*Nyctalus noctula* Schreber) occurs over England and Wales, and in most of Scotland, living mainly in woodland. Natterer's bat (*Selysius nattereri* Kuhl), found over most of Britain, prefers park land and woodland that is fairly open. You might see the tiny pipistrelle (*Pipistrellus pipistrellus* Schreber), or in England – but not Scotland or Wales – the barbastelle (*Barbastella barbastella* Schreber). It is slightly larger than the pipistrelle and seems to prefer wooded river valleys where it can fly low over the water in its hunt for insects.

Much of the diversity of life in mature woodland, apart from the trees themselves and the larger plants, is hidden; you may hear the cry of birds, or glimpse a squirrel, but it requires time, patience, and some cunning to discover more. If you are lucky, an early morning or late afternoon walk through a wood may bring you a sight of badgers or a fox. Yet whether you see them or not they are there, members of a living community, comprising a system complete unto itself, in which little is wasted.

The removal of the trees destroys the system. Many of the species

147

making up the community are dispersed or killed. That is what 'habitat destruction' means, and there is more to restoring a habitat than simply replacing its more conspicuous components. Nothing lives in isolation and you cannot make a woodland merely by planting trees. The trees dominate the area they occupy, but they do so by virtue of the collaboration of countless billions of organisms, many of them so small you need a powerful microscope to see them at all. These tiny organisms constantly recycle the nutrients by which the trees grow, and the trees in turn provide space, shelter and food for many more plants and animals. A woodland is a community, not only trees.

You may supply the trees and wait to see whether and how quickly a rich woodland community develops; or – simpler and much more reliable – you may retain mature woodland which exists already.

9
Conserving Woodland

Even when we take account of the large Forestry Commission plantations established since the 1920s, Britain has less forest and woodland than most countries. Some 9 per cent of our land area is wooded (2018 thousand hectares, comprising 855 thousand hectares in England, 234 thousand hectares in Wales, and 929 thousand hectares in Scotland). In Japan the figure is around 60 per cent.

We inherited a small area, of course, from the original clearance 2,000 years ago, but we have cleared more. In the last thirty years we have inflicted more extensive and more serious damage on our woodlands than during any similar period in modern history, perhaps than in any similar period at any time. Our change is of a different order, a different quality. When farming was deeply depressed and farmers faced bankruptcy, often they would fell some trees to bring in a little much-needed cash. This amounted to a lot of felling in a short time, but the trees recovered, or new trees grew, and in time the woodland returned. The use of the land had not changed; and that is the difference.

The removal of woodland and hedges since the 1950s has not been forced on landowners by poverty, or to realise capital. It has been a means to gain better access to the land and to free more land for cultivation. The process is a repetition of the original clearances in its association with the expansion of agriculture: woodland has been converted into farm land. Where it has been replaced, usually the replacement has consisted of plantation, with a strong preference for conifers. Even isolated trees have been replaced, if at all, by exotic species or by conifers when they died. The change has repeated the change made in Roman and pre-Roman times, but it started from a much lower base, and its effects have been dramatic.

It has become fashionable to rail against the farmer and the forester. The farmer especially is presented as an avaricious,

Winter is the time for maintenance work on farms, and this includes laying hedges, a craft that is alive and well, despite fears that it might disappear. Hedge-laying styles vary from one part of the country to another. This hedge is in Worcestershire. The thicker stems of the hawthorn have been cut almost through, and the trees bent over and pegged in position, while smaller wood has been woven along the top from stake to stake. In spring the trees will start to grow again and soon the hedge will support a rich community of plants and animals, while remaining stock-proof. It will be years before such a well-laid hedge needs laying again, and until then maintenance will be minimal (*Mr & Mrs R. P. Lawrence/Frank Lane Agency*)

insensitive figure, waxing rich on state subsidies awarded for the despoliation of the countryside. Like all extreme statements, this one obscures the truth rather than illuminating it. If we must have scapegoats, we may all of us be implicated.

The removal of woodland has accompanied the 'modernisation' of farming. Clearly the two are linked, but the link is more subtle than it may appear. It has two strands, one economic, the other related to our concept of land-use planning. During the 1939–45 war, when for the second time this century a serious attempt was made to blockade this country, the British might have starved. Agriculture was so depressed in the late 1930s, so under-developed, that it was poorly equipped to feed us. Rationing was introduced, emergency measures were taken to boost farm output, and we survived. At the end of the war there was general agreement that for strategic reasons the output from British farms had to be increased much further, and that farming had to become economically secure. Only with such security could the industry attract the investment it needed so desperately.

A complex package of economic support measures was devised, comprising grants for particular kinds of farm improvement, subsidies on the use of certain materials, notably fertilisers, and – the most vital component of the package – guaranteed prices, which ensured that if farmers responded to the other measures and increased output, they would not suffer from a drop in prices. When Britain entered the European Economic Community the method of support changed, but the principle remained. The Common Agricultural Policy aims to produce a modern, efficient, highly productive agricultural industry, very largely by providing it with economic stability.

In the 1950s, the success of the new regime was phenomenal. Output rose very rapidly indeed, from a low starting point, and the government found itself spending vast sums of money to support farm prices. There was a brief period of 'feather-bedding' when many farmers really did grow wealthy, but it did not last. The government responded to it by increasing the agreed support prices each year, at an annual review, by an amount slightly smaller than the annual increase in costs; so to maintain their incomes, farmers had to produce more each year. They were squeezed, and the squeeze has continued.

It led to increased capital investment, as was intended. It led to an increase in the use of fertiliser, as was intended, until with some crops the point was reached where any further raising of yields would need more spent on fertiliser than the value of the additional

152

crop. It led to greater mechanisation, with a consequent shedding of manpower, and to the greater use of pesticides to reduce crop losses in the field. It also led to greater and greater specialisation, which concentrated the livestock enterprises in the west of the country and the arable enterprises in the drier, sunnier east.

It increased the value of farm land, which in the 1930s could be bought for £10 an acre. In March 1983 the average price for farm land in Britain stood at a little over £1,400 an acre. For most of the time, land values rose faster than the rate of inflation. It is this increase more than anything which makes farmers seem wealthy. A farmer with a little more than 700 acres of reasonable land is a millionaire. Yet the millionaire may live like a peasant, because he cannot spend his money. He must live on the proceeds from the food he sells. The wealth is much more apparent than real.

In the continuing struggle to maintain or increase incomes during a time of rising land prices, it makes economic sense to plough every corner of every farm; the crop from the new land means income, and the improvement of the land increases its value. As a group, farmers are no greedier than the rest of us, but it has been difficult for them to resist the temptation to clear unprofitable woodland in order to grow crops or graze stock. They are as much victims as villains, and if we must have scapegoats we should search among those who designed the farm-support system and failed to predict all its consequences. We might also look at those who interpret the system to farmers, especially now that the EEC provides alternatives to the perpetual intensification of farming which we ignore.

At about the time the farm-support system was being designed, we were also planning a comprehensive machine for planning the way land in Britain is used. The idea was to prevent the expansion of towns on to farm land, to prevent ribbon development which was considered too unsightly, and to set aside large tracts of land in which the public might relax, calling them National Parks. British 'National Parks' do not conform to the international definition of National Parks, which requires them to be wilderness areas, not 'parks' at all; but the British coined the name first, and we continue to use it in our own way.

The planning system did not cover land used for farming or forestry. It was argued that our landscape, the landscape which we aimed to protect through wise planning, had been created by farmers and foresters. They were preserving for us what we wished to preserve, and therefore could be appointed guardians of the rural landscape. We could not at the same time subject them to planning controls.

As farming and forestry developed in directions toward which they were forced by their own economic planners, conservationists began to question the wisdom of that original decision, but by then it was too late. Not only had much of the damage been done, but the planning of the use of rural land had grown extremely complex. Local planning authorities regulated some building, mainly to prevent any increase in the number of people dwelling in the countryside. The Ministry of Defence, which owns large areas of land, pursued its own objectives, beyond the reach of any planners but its own. Water authorities sought to prevent farming close to their reservoirs, for fear of pollution of the water. The Forestry Commission, the Ministry of Agriculture, Fisheries & Food, National Park authorities, the Countryside Commission, the Nature Conservancy (which later became the Nature Conservancy Council), all had objectives of their own, all had opinions of their own about how best to protect wildlife and landscapes, and all went their own ways. The incoherence of the resultant planning system will be difficult to untangle. Voluntary conservation and amenity groups, some of which owned land and some of which did not, as well as the National Trust, which owns land in a legally peculiar way, campaigned, complained, argued and could make little headway.

When we consider ways to conserve woodland, therefore, we approach a very complex situation, and no single solution will be adequate. We must encourage new planting, of course, but of broadleaved woodland rather than forest plantation. We must try to inculcate new ways of thinking about the countryside, and about woodland in particular. Through education and persuasion we must try to convince people that the future of the countryside is a matter for general concern. It involves, or should involve, all of us, and unless we understand the problem and care enough to contribute to its solution, its development may continue in a piecemeal, haphazard fashion, toward an end of which we would not approve.

The protection of such woodland as remains sounds simple. You identify an area of woodland, draw a line around it on the map, and forbid anyone to interfere with it. But that does not work. In the first place all land is owned by someone, and the agreement of the owner must be sought. Many owners would agree, but even that offers little real security. All land is owned, and all landowners are mortal. What will happen to the woodland when the present owner sells it or dies?

Perhaps we can protect it legally? Already it is possible to place preservation orders on individual trees, or on areas of woodland, and vast numbers of trees are 'protected' in this way. The preservation orders are issued by local authorities, and since their budgets have been reduced they have become a little reluctant to issue more. They must pay compensation to the landowner for each order they issue, if the owner claims that by not felling a tree income has been lost, which can get expensive. Still, the orders exist, and so does the machinery for issuing more of them. Yet they are negative. Many Woodland Trust woods are covered by tree preservation orders. The Trust cannot claim that any loss of income is incurred through not felling them, and so it receives no payment. Conservation will be paid for only as a last resort to protect what would otherwise be lost.

A landowner who fells protected trees without obtaining a licence to do so can be prosecuted and fined. The trouble is that it may well be more profitable to pay the fine than to preserve the trees. To raise the fine to a truly punitive level would cause bitter resentment and would not meet the case. Enforcing draconian measures against landowners who really were compelled financially to clear woodland might be impossible. They might have to sell land to pay their debts – or to pay the fine – and we might find ourselves back where we started. Their best course might be to fell the trees in order to increase the value of the land to be sold, and thus pay both creditor and fine, perhaps with a small amount left.

Areas can be designated for protection, as Sites of Special Scientific Interest (SSSI). This is a planning procedure under which the Secretary of State for the Environment, and the Secretaries of State for Scotland and Wales, acting on the advice of the Nature Conservancy Council, impose special controls on activities that would alter areas of particular biological, ecological or geological value. Similar protection is afforded to sites of archaeological importance. In practice this does not always work; the requirement that landowners must receive special permission before altering an area of Special Scientific Interest is almost impossible to enforce. The Nature Conservancy Council, overworked and under-funded, has the greatest difficulty in supervising the sites with which it is concerned – even in recording them accurately – and by the time it hears that a site is in danger it is often too late, sometimes years too late.

The Wildlife and Countryside Act 1981 aimed to resolve many of the difficulties, but it has proved unpopular among conservationists, and costly because of its requirement that landowners be compensated financially for income lost when they are forbidden to destroy valuable habitat. The compensation sounds fair, but no money was made available to finance it. The Nature Conservancy Council was held responsible for that. Situations could and did arise when

155

landowners were being told by government agricultural advisers of ways to change their farming methods in order to increase the profitability of their holdings, while government conservation advisers were urging them to leave things as they were in the interests of habitat protection.

What is worse, farmers in some areas announced plans to destroy habitat, and so claimed compensation for not doing so, even though they had farmed the land for years without feeling any need to make the changes they now proposed: it looked very much as though they saw the provisions of the Act as a source of unearned income. The income may be considerable, since it is calculated at so much an acre a year for many years.

So the Act is a nonsense? That, certainly, is the view of many people, although there is some hope that it will be revised and improved in the not too distant future. It is not entirely futile, of course. The comprehensive lists of plants and animals afforded statutory protection are accepted in general though a few of the provisions seem draconian: if you found, say, a feather from any bird mentioned in the schedules, theoretically you would commit an offence if you picked it up and took it home.

Even the concept of compensation may be more subtle and more interesting than it seems at first glance. It depends on what you suppose its purpose to be. If you think it exists simply in order to pay landowners for not damaging conservation interests, then it does indeed look like a crude bribe, expensive and in the end unworkable. But there is another view. If you believe that Britain now produces more food than it needs and should not seek ever greater output, and that the wish to reduce timber imports by increasing domestic production can be pursued too far, to the detriment of landscapes and the natural environment, then you are urging the imposition of restrictions on the economic activities of landowners – and, through that, on people who live in rural areas. If you think the reforms conservationists desire should not lead to economic hardship among country dwellers and the further decline of rural communities, then other ways have to be found to bring employment and income into the countryside. If people are to earn less from farming and forestry, if these industries are to provide fewer jobs, then we must find other ways for people to earn their livings.

When landowners are awarded compensation for not causing environmental damage, it is not money for doing nothing that they should receive. The compensation must be conditional upon the agreement and implementation of a management plan, and that means the landowner must actually manage the area in certain ways. The landowner, then, agrees to abandon one course of action in favour of another, and is paid for the positive actions he or she takes in the interests of the environment; those actions are specified clearly and supervised.

This introduces a new concept, and one that conservationists might welcome. Landowners are to be employed on supervised conservation work, so providing local employment and preventing economic decline in rural areas, while enhancing the environment. The amounts may have been calculated wrongly, the details may be capable of refinement, the entire means of financing the scheme may be wrong, but the principles may deserve conservationist support.

If finance is the main problem, it should be feasible to fund the system within existing budgets and without bankrupting the Nature Conservancy Council. Since both farming and forestry depend on public subsidy, a part of that subsidy might be redirected. Farmers could be paid to retain woodland. Then we – the taxpayers – might feel entitled to be a little more specific about the way in which the woodland should be retained; it might be possible to reinstate its management. The National Trust, for example, owns woodland on some of its estates which it manages primarily for amenity purposes, but such woodland management does imply an economic return, a crop. The subsidy might not have to be as large as it seems at first sight.

It would help greatly if markets could be developed for woodland produce and products, ideally through partnerships between local craft industries and landowners, perhaps based on coppice wood. Even fuelwood may have a value, although wood-burning stoves, so beloved of the ethnic set, have a strong claim to being the most dangerously polluting devices ever invented. Ironically, it is their 'efficiency' which makes them dangerous: because they burn wood slowly, at relatively low temperatures, they emit unburned hydro-carbon compounds as well as the more usual products of combustion. These compounds comprise a list of poisons including several substances believed to cause cancer. Even a coal fire is cleaner! Yet there could be a substantial amount of useful fuel available. Some years ago, for example, I calculated that if hedgerow trimmings could be collected, chopped and packed on farms for sale as fuel, the total national yield might be equivalent to about 18 million tons of coal a year. That is a lot of coal, and most decidedly has a value. Provided it was burned efficiently – quickly and at high tempera-tures – it should not cause much pollution. If you wish to preserve something, making it more valuable is a help. A sale for the

Coppicing provides a perpetual supply of small wood. In the past it was used for fuel and for making many articles in daily use. Today wood from this sweet-chestnut coppice is split to make palings (*M. Nimmo/Frank Lane Agency*)

trimmings might make the removal of hedges a little less attractive economically.

From a conservation point of view the first and by far the most important and urgent priority is to prevent the further loss of old woodland, and especially of ancient woodland. Any scheme that might help, might allow us to pay for the retention of woodland, needs very serious consideration.

Planting too is important since it is an obviously practicable way to increase the total area of woodland, and the number of trees. It is not the only way possible. If land is abandoned, left to be colonised in its own time and its own way, much of it reverts to woodland. Perhaps we might identify areas in which just this should be allowed to happen.

There is more to planting a tree than the scattering of acorns on the ground, just as there are more kinds of tree than oak. Similarly, there is more to creating new woodland than planting trees. We have tried exhortation. We even had a 'Plant a Tree' year, in 1973: the theory, I suppose, was that if one tree was planted by or on behalf of every man, woman and child in Britain, that would be some 60 million trees put in, all in one year. For a moment, the attention of the nation was turned to tree planting, and on sunny days little groups would gather and have a ceremony. But the mortality rate among newly planted trees can be high, especially when they are planted in the wrong place, at the wrong time and under the wrong conditions, as too many of these were. Many of the trees were exotics – flowering cherries, eucalypts, cedars, and a lot of red maples, magnolias and tulip trees; also lots and lots of oak. They were planted in gardens, beside the road, on waste ground, in parks, indeed all over towns. Then they were abandoned – and many of them died. People forgot about them and gave up planting trees.

The exhortation did a little good, but on balance it may have done more harm, because it concentrated on trees rather than on woodland. There is nothing wrong with planting exotic trees in the right places; they are attractive and interesting, and the British have a long tradition of collecting plants from every corner of the world. Only it is not exotics that we need so badly. Nor is there anything wrong with planting native species such as oak in our gardens or around our towns, provided the sites are suitable for them. There was, though, no need to persuade the British that trees are beautiful, and enhance the human environment. They have always known that.

What we need now is not trees, but woodland. For that, we must plan carefully, set land aside, prepare the ground, select the species, and after planting, tend them. It demands continuing commitment, and it costs money. Not all of us can participate directly, or would wish to, but in one way or another those of us who enjoy woodland must make it possible for woodland to be created.

We must proceed on several fronts: first, foremost, and most urgently by encouraging the retention of existing old woodland, then by new planting, but at the same time by revising our concepts of the countryside. We must avoid vague sentimentality, especially as this manifests itself in the two most commonly held and opposing points of view – that our countryside is either 'natural' or 'man-made'. It is both and it is neither. It is the product of a long and not always happy partnership between humans and non-humans. We must rewrite the terms of that partnership agreement.

This calls for a shift in our values and our perception of our long-term interest. The *World Conservation Strategy*, published by the International Union for Conservation of Nature and Natural Resources, the UN Environment Programme, and the World Wildlife Fund, in collaboration with several other UN agencies,

159

defined those values in general terms at the international level. More recently, *The Conservation and Development Programme for the UK* has related the *Strategy* to Britain. The conservationist view expressed in these documents is gaining support rapidly in industry and government. It suggests that everything we use, including air, water, soil and the countryside itself, should be regarded as resources in the traditional sense of that word, and that our use of resources should aim to be sustainable. An activity which destroys the resources on which it depends cannot continue indefinitely.

Our countryside exists as a whole, and it serves many purposes beyond the production of food and raw materials. It provides amenity, and habitats for our wildlife; and woodland is especially important for both. When we lose woodland we are impoverished. We need woodland, then, as well as productive plantation forest, and there is nothing wrong with placing an equal value on both, each for its own reason. While the forest produces timber, the broadleaved woodland contributes to the richness of our countryside, and our lives.

We need both, we can have both, but how are we to achieve so desirable a goal? The necessary change of view must be the result of the national debate that is taking place about the future of the countryside. Eventually it may be possible to modify the planning system and permit the emergence of a single, coherent policy of rural land use. That will be of great value, but it may come too late. Conservationists cannot pause in their efforts, in the hope of brighter times to come, lest what they seek to conserve in the long term be lost in the short term. While we are agreeing the best way to conserve woods in general, who is it that is seeking to conserve this or that wood in particular, and how may we best help them?

10
How to save a wood

 Historically, the clearance of British woodlands has proceeded in two distinct phases. The first and largest, had ended probably by Saxon times. One of its effects was to stimulate interest in the conservation of woodlands, and this was followed by the development of a high standard of woodland management.

The second phase began around 1950, and is continuing still. It is in this short time that the conservationist has come to be seen, by some people, as eccentric, and that the conservation movement has had to become more forceful to be heard. We can do nothing about clearances made 2,000 years ago, but we must seize any chance to halt and even reverse the present clearances. We must not criticise woodland conservationists for being strident, for their cause is urgent. Least of all should we, as conservationists, be disheartened by allegations that woodland conservation is out of tune with the times. It is the times which are out of tune with history. The arguments in favour of retaining woodlands are strong, and they also express the traditionally British view; until very recently the British would go to great lengths to protect woodlands. It is those who would plough, graze or concrete every last patch of copse who are doing violence to our traditions. Happily, if you reveal your wish to protect a wood there are many people who will be willing to help.

If your concern is for woodlands in general, rather than for a particular woodland area which you know and believe to be threatened, then support an appropriate conservation organisation. The most obvious choice is the Woodland Trust. Employing a small permanent staff, it has its own professional support, augmented occasionally by outside specialists, and receives financial support from the Countryside Commission, the Nature Conservancy Council and the World Wildlife Fund, as well as many local authorities and numerous other bodies and individuals. Almost every penny it receives is used to buy threatened woodland. The Trust believes that a woodland, and especially one which has occupied the same site for centuries or millennia, perhaps since the last ice advance, is as much a part of our national heritage as is a fine stately home, a medieval castle or a great work of art. It belongs to us, in the sense that it is part of us, part of our history. Yet woodland enjoys little formal protection. The only sure way to protect it is to own it. The Trust opens most of its woodlands to the public, providing an amenity from which formerly they may have been excluded.

If you own woodland and wish to see it retained and well managed, after you have ceased to be able to care for it yourself, the Trust will become your steward. It has acquired many areas of woodland by such gift. Even if the land is not wooded, the Trust would be glad of it, for then it could be planted, to become woodland for the future. There is no area too small to be of interest and value; a single small field can be used. The Trust will admit the public to your wood unless there is a compelling reason not to do so – while new trees are becoming established, for example.

The Trust was founded in 1972. It is young – many conservation bodies are much older. During its short life, however, it has enjoyed a success nothing short of phenomenal. It is one of the fastest-growing conservation bodies in Britain, and in terms of membership is now one of the largest. It has found a response in that eternal British love of woodland.

It was started by one man, as are so many voluntary societies. Kenneth Watkins began with the purchase of about 100 acres beside the River Avon, in the South Hams area of South Devon, not far from his own home. Before long the Trust was managing woods in many parts of England and Wales. In 1982, at the end of its first ten years, the Trust owned 79 woods, in 23 counties, covering more than 2,000 acres. That made it one of the country's largest non-commercial owners of woodland. More recently it has acquired its first woods in Scotland. Its growth continues, and in the year ending October 1982 it spent more than half a million pounds, buying woods at the rate of one a month. Over four years it increased its membership from 1,000 to 20,000, and it raised more than £1.5 million. By the winter of 1984 membership stood at 40,000, and new members were joining at a rate of 300 a week. It managed 130 woods, with a total area of 4,000 acres, and on average was acquiring a new wood every two weeks. Yet it can still promise new members that £1 of their first subscription will be spent on planting a tree, and most of the remainder will help to purchase and care for land.

162

Once bought, of course, woodland must be managed, and this may mean departing from the way it has been managed in the past. If a wood contains only one or two species, having been commercial plantation at one time, it may be desirable to introduce more trees. It may be necessary to increase the density of trees, to allow coppiced trees to grow into standards, or to start coppicing. Fences may need mending, paths opening, gates and stiles repairing, and a warden will be needed to keep an eye on everything day by day. Wardens are usually local volunteers who superintend woods in their spare time.

As an individual, or a member of a local conservation group, you can seek help in protecting a particular piece of woodland that you know and which you believe may be threatened. Like any other wildlife habitat, a wood must be assessed to discover what lives there, and to discover whether it has any feature of particular scientific or historical interest. This is a specialised task, but there is no shortage of people able to undertake it. As an individual you could get in touch with the nearest regional office of the Nature Conservancy Council, or with your county trust for nature con- servation. (Both of these are listed in the telephone directory.) Either body, or the two of them working in collaboration, as they often do, will provide the scientific expertise, and will be quick to identify anything unusual or rare.

If the wood is of some scientific importance, the Nature Con- servancy Council might even wish to designate it a Site of Special Scientific Interest (SSSI) – although this affords only limited protection, as explained in chapter 9.

If the site is scientifically valuable and the owner wishes, or agrees, to see it preserved, it might become a nature reserve. National Nature Reserves are designated and managed by the Nature Conservancy Council. The land may become Crown pro- perty, may be leased to the Council, or may be managed by the Council by agreement. Alternatively, it may become a Local Nature Reserve. There are not so many of these; most are designated and then managed by local authorities.

The third alternative is to make the land into a less formal kind of reserve, under the auspices of a conservation body and managed by volunteers.

Once a way has been found to ensure the future of the wood, something must be done with it. Usually it will require no special treatment, beyond good traditional management, which involves a great deal of hard manual work. Volunteers can be found who will gladly devote long, enjoyable but laborious hours to this, and will often bring formidable skills to their tasks.

The Council for Nature, an umbrella organisation to bring together the many bodies involved in nature conservation, was formed in 1958. It has been absorbed into the Council for Environmental Conservation (CoEnCo). A year after it formed, believing that many young people might welcome an opportunity to work on conservation projects, the Council formed the Conservation Corps, led by a retired army officer, Brigadier E.F.E. Armstrong. The response was good, and in its first year the Corps worked more than 1,000 man-days. Most Corps members were students, none of them below the age of sixteen, their average age being twenty. Tasks were organised for weekends and during academic vacations. After he 'retired' in 1965, Brig Armstrong helped his own county trust for nature conservation to form a local conservation corps in Gloucestershire, to help in the management of the county nature reserves. The Corps grew, but was always hampered by lack of funds, and by 1967 was facing likely closure. Although the members received no payment, they had to be supplied with tools, equipment and transport, and their work had to be supervised.

It was in 1967 that the Soil Association stepped in to help. The Association, concerned mainly with the reform of farming methods, had received much financial assistance from a charitable trust, and was able both to make funds available to the Corps and to initiate a project which brought Corps teams on to farm land to manage areas of habitat there. The Soil Association and the Council for Nature formed a joint committee to manage the Corps and to prepare it for relaunching as the British Trust for Conservation Volunteers. That came into being in 1970. Since then its work has expanded, it has opened regional offices in several parts of the country, and Conservation Volunteers have worked in many Woodland Trust woods.

The help given by the volunteers amounts to much more than mere labour, for it is an aim of the BTCV to provide training. There is a strong educational component in its activities, and it can advise on the practical aspects of implementing a management programme. While it conserves habitats for wildlife it also tries to keep alive traditional rural crafts; members are taught how to use tools which have been refined and perfected over millennia, but which could disappear to museums as machines take over their tasks – often very approximately. Thus the collaboration of the BTCV can mean that a sensible management programme is devised, and then applied properly, by people who know what they are doing.

There may be different reasons for wishing to conserve a wood. An

164

isolated plantation on top of a hill may be very important visually. Local people may know and love it: it forms a familiar part of their world. Yet it will provide a poor habitat for wildlife. It is an 'oasis', and will support more plants and animals than an arable field, for example, or a field of pasture sown with rye grass, but as no routes, no hedgerows, link it with other woodland, it is poorer than most woods. You might therefore think its loss would not be serious. Nearby farmers might regret losing sight of it, but would welcome the departure of the rooks and wood-pigeons which roost in it.

All the same, the voices of the people who live within sight of the wood and enjoy walking in it must be heard; any loss of woodland must be regarded as serious. If at all possible the wood should be retained, for apart from anything else its appearance and its value as habitat can be improved. If the wood, any wood, is retained, then sooner or later it will need attention. Dead wood may have to be removed, new trees planted to compensate for losses. The necessary management will provide opportunities to improve the wood visually, or as habitat for wildlife.

It may be necessary to alter the composition of a wood. A stand of pure sycamore or oak, for example, will depress smaller shrubs and herbs, both by casting shade and also because these leaves rot very slowly and tend to lie on top of small plants, suppressing them. The introduction of other tree species might permit more of the smaller plants to thrive.

A wood may be of special historical interest, or of great amenity value. In most of the upland areas of Britain the high moors are bisected by narrow, steep-sided valleys, where woodland thrives in the shelter of the surrounding high ground, and where a river completes the scene. Almost invariably such valleys are popular local beauty spots. Too steep to be cultivable, and not needed for sheep, they offer 'spare' land, and farmers as much as anyone else enjoy the tranquility they find there. Such valleys are not threatened with development, but unless their wooded slopes regenerate naturally, in time the woodland may be lost, or may change in ways which make it less attractive. The woods may not need protection, but they do need management.

(overleaf)
River valleys often provide sheltered sites on land that slopes too steeply to be of much use to farmers; here trees can be allowed to flourish. Avon Woods, in South Devon, extend for about 2 miles along the banks of the Avon as a winding belt of woodland that provides a delightful riverside walk and also adds visual interest to the otherwise agricultural landscape (*Nicholas Horne/The Woodland Trust*)

Many of the woods lying on more open ground in the uplands are threatened, because they are not fenced securely to keep out grazing sheep, and on the lower ground even cattle, which can prevent regeneration by destroying seedlings.

The British countryside is very diverse, and it is dangerous to make general statements about it. Some years ago there was much discussion about the meaning of the word 'conservation'. If it meant 'preservation', it was argued, we might be trying to turn rural Britain into some kind of museum, to freeze its development and hold it perpetually at some arbitrarily chosen historical point. This might appeal to some town-dwellers, but it would be resisted strenuously by people who live in the countryside and who do not see themselves as museum attendants. So it was proposed that conservation must mean the best, most thrifty use of resources. That, farmers might protest, is precisely the way they and the foresters use rural resources, so the most effective form of conservation would be to leave them alone to get on with it. Perhaps there is something not quite right about the definition!

Recently it has been suggested that the countryside, as an abstract aesthetic concept, is the property of the nation as a whole, and that the nation as a whole should be responsible for its maintenance. It should be adapted to serve the widest possible range of interests. Since agriculture has been so successful in increasing output, and since European agriculture suffers at the moment more from food surpluses than from shortages, agriculture might be scaled down in favour of more tourism and more amenity use, especially of the rural lowlands. Again, the proposal overlooks the preferences of the people who live in the countryside and who must earn a living there. It tends toward the rural museum once more, and in any case it would be difficult to implement without the high cost of taking large areas of land into public ownership.

Probably our difficulties derive from our attempts to generalise. Nowhere can the problems be seen more clearly than with woodlands. There is no overall rule. There are woodlands of such scientific or historical interest that most of us would agree they should be retained as they are. If this turns them into museum exhibits, so be it. If we can justify the restoration of abandoned factories for use as industrial museums, why should we not convert some woodlands into museums? There are woodlands which deserve protection for their scenic value. We have art galleries in which great paintings are displayed, and no one seems to object that the gallery site might be used more profitably for offices or flats. Why should we not have 'rural galleries'? 'Preservation' can be justified, but in particular cases only, not in general. Elsewhere, woodlands should be allowed to develop under proper management. This safeguards the woodland, but does not preserve it in unchanged form. It amounts to the wise, thrifty use of a resource, and corresponds to the alternative definition of 'conservation'.

Landowners have objected that those who demand conservation should find ways to pay for it. If we allow the land to be managed commercially then particular landscapes will develop. If we accept that landowners usually manage their holdings in the most profitable way, then it follows that any alternative system of management would be less profitable. That is what they mean. Conservationists may have to grasp the nettle and admit that if we want a countryside different from the purely commercial one, finance will have to be found. Now, though, it may be that we have found it, in the form of the support to agriculture and forestry that could be diverted, not to different recipients, but to the same recipients for different purposes.

So if you know a wood which you believe to be threatened, people with diverse skills in assessment and planning are needed before firm decisions can be reached. Try to find out whether the threat is real or just rumour: there have been cases of protest campaigns mounted on the basis of rumours, and of landowners being urged vehemently to protect woodland they had not considered harming. It is as well to be sure of the facts, and not to put ideas into people's heads! Such misinformed campaigns may serve to fire warning shots and to demonstrate the strength of feeling, but they may also waste time and effort. Should the threat prove real, then by all means form a group to investigate the nature of the threat, to alert the local planning authority, and to draw public attention to the matter.

Then contact the Woodland Trust. There are many conservation organisations active in rural affairs, but it is the Trust which specialises in the problems affecting woodland. It has the experience to be able to give sound advice, the respect of academic and statutory bodies which give it access to specialist help and to such grants as may be available; and yet it remains independent of outside influences and pressures.

If there is no woodland near you, or no woodland in danger of being cleared, then join the Trust anyway. It costs little, and your subscription will help others whose woods are threatened, and help to buy, restore or plant woodland in other parts of the country.

At present, the conservation of British woodland, however you may define 'conservation', is something of an emergency operation. With your help it could proceed just a little faster.

Directory of Woodlands

The aim of this book has been to describe woodlands, to encourage their conservation, and to show the desirability of increasing our national woodland area. If it attains those objectives it will have succeeded, but only partially. To appreciate woodland fully, you need to visit it, walk in it and experience it for yourself.

The woodland areas in the list which follows are those which belong to or are managed by the Woodland Trust, the National Trust, the Forestry Commission, or by county trusts for nature conservation, or which are National Nature Reserves. All the areas managed by the Woodland Trust when the list was compiled are included, but the list dates rapidly because of the Trust's frequent acquisitions. Some of these are important examples of particular types of woodland; others are included simply because they are attractive, or of local interest, or because they illustrate types of woodland or management practices described earlier in this book. The list does not pretend to be a complete inventory of woods owned or managed by county trusts.

Most of the woods are open to the public, but access to many National Nature Reserves, and to a small number of other woods, is restricted. Some National Nature Reserves are owned or leased by the Nature Conservancy Council, but many are established under nature reserve agreements with owners or occupiers. All National Nature Reserves are protected, and part of that protection in some cases entails limiting the number of visitors who walk around them at any particular time, so you may need an entry permit – obtainable from the regional office of the Nature Conservancy Council. The addresses of the county trusts for nature conservation, and of the regional offices of the Nature Conservancy Council, are listed in the local telephone directories. If you plan to visit a wood for which a permit is needed, and which is beyond the range of your local directory, then telephone the nearest office and ask for the number to contact.

The National Trust may charge non-members a fee for admission to some of its woodlands.

171

Each wood can be located from its national grid reference.

If you are not an experienced visitor of woods, or any other part of the countryside, remember that the species you enjoy can be harmed. Do not light fires. Do not leave litter. Do not make unnecessary noise. Do not pollute water. Close gates. If you must cross land on which farm animals are kept, make sure that you do not frighten them. In particular, if you have a dog, keep it on the lead and firmly under control. Keep to footpaths unless this is obviously impossible, and where paths cross field or other boundaries use the stile or gate. Such commonsense precautions help to protect the countryside from you. Also be prepared to protect yourself from it! Beware of old mine-workings or overgrown quarries, which may lie as traps for the unwary. Woodland footpaths may call for strong, comfortable, waterproof boots or shoes. Take waterproof outer clothes. Carry a good map, and know how to read it. Finally, if you plan to visit a remote area, tell someone you can trust where you are going, your route, and when you expect to return.

AVON

Bishops Knoll Grid reference ST553753. 6 acres. At the western end of the Avon Gorge, very close to Bristol, overlooking the river. The wood has many mature trees as well as areas planted in 1984. Owned by the Woodland Trust. The Bristol City Council is collaborating with the Trust in improving access by linking the footpaths.

Chivers Knoll Grid reference ST657569. 0.5 acre. Originally the spoil-heap from a small coal mine which was worked briefly, probably in the eighteenth century, and forms a prominent landmark on the edge of Paulton. Owned by the Woodland Trust.

Upton Cheyney Grid reference ST701702. 7 acres. Between Keynsham and Bath. The area comprises three fields which have been planted by the Woodland Trust under a 'Create a Wood' scheme. The land is not owned by the Trust, but is held on a long lease.

BUCKINGHAMSHIRE

Chalkdell Wood Grid reference SP900012. 2.5 acres. Situated within the Chiltern Area of Outstanding Natural Beauty, near Great Missenden, this wood is typical of Chiltern beechwoods. Owned by the Woodland Trust.

Chesham Bois Wood Grid reference SP960003. 40 acres. On the edge of the Chiltern Area of Outstanding Natural Beauty, between Chesham and Amersham, this high forest of beech acts as a buffer between two urban areas and is much used by local people. Beech timber is still used locally by furniture factories. Lying on a shallow soil overlying chalk, the wood contains many species of flowering plants, at their best in early summer, before the tree canopy closes to shade them. Car access is easy as the wood lies to either side of the A416 road, and it is within walking distance of both Chesham and Amersham Underground stations (Metropolitan Line). Owned by the Woodland Trust.

Tenterden Spinney Grid reference SU967995. 5 acres. The spinney, in this case a small wood, comprises mixed woodland with a path through the centre. Surrounded by houses, close to Chesham Bois, it is locally popular. Owned by the Woodland Trust.

CAMBRIDGESHIRE

Aversley Wood Grid reference TL158815. 152 acres – one of the larger woods in the county. Ancient, most of it dating back to the start of the present interglacial, it contains wild service trees, which are found only in ancient woodland, and it also illustrates the coppice-with-standards system of management. There are plans to reintroduce coppicing. The wood contains some areas of pure hazel, and others with a mixture of hazel, ash, and field maple; also some oak. In 1979 Dutch elm disease killed the elms which occupied one area, which has now been cleared. Ash will predominate unless its regeneration is reduced by management. The black hairstreak butterfly (*Strymonidia pruni*) has been recorded there, in a large area of blackthorns, and in spring the wood is noted for its bluebells. There are three ponds, one being an armed pond, uncommon in this part of the country. At the southern end, about 50 acres lies on land which bears clearly the ridge-and-furrow marks of former ploughing. The wood is owned by the Woodland Trust and is a Site of Special Scientific Interest. Controlled shooting takes place in the wood on four days in the year, so before a visit it would be best to check first with the Trust office (telephone 0476 74297). The wood is situated just west of the A1 road, south of the village of Sawtry. Access is by a bridleway across the fields from Hill Top Farm (south-east of the wood) The path was once part of the Bullock Road droveway. The wood can also be reached from Sawtry village.

Hayley Wood Grid reference TL295536. 122 acres. Lying on the Cambridgeshire boulder clay at Little Gransden, and with 700 years of recorded history, this wood consists mainly of standard oak, with coppiced ash, field maple, and hazel in part of the wood where the county trust has reintroduced the traditional management system. There are many species of flowering plants and birds. It is a nature reserve owned and managed by the county trust for nature conservation. Access, for pedestrians only, is along Hayley Lane from its junction with the St Neots to Barton Road (B1046) nearly 2 miles west of the junction with the A14 at Longstowe. Access is by permit only and permits for non-members can be obtained from Cambient, 1 Brookside, Cambridge.

Wicken Fen Grid reference TL563705. 600 acres. Situated 3 miles west of Soham and 17 miles north-east of Cambridge, with the main entrance in Lode Lane, Wicken, Ely. The area contains alder buckthorn woodland and wetland, an undrained remnant of the Great Fens, and supports many species of plants and animals. It is a nature reserve owned by the National Trust, and is open every day of the year. Parties admitted by arrangement with the Warden, Warden's House, Wicken Fen, Lode Lane, Wicken, Ely, Cambs, CB7 5XP (or telephone Ely 720274). There is a charge for the admission of non-members.

CLWYD

Bigwood Grid reference SJ188675. 21 acres. Situated on a hillside over the A541 road between Mold and Denbigh, near the village of Hendre. A mature wood dominated by oak and ash, the best example in the area of this type of woodland on a limestone soil. Owned by the Woodland Trust.

Coed Tyddyn halen Grid reference SJ155725. 7 acres. Eight miles from Mold, this is a secluded wood containing a wide variety of trees and shrubs. It has been disturbed little, and has a rich ground flora. There is also a fast-flowing stream and a marshy area. Owned by the Woodland Trust.

CORNWALL

Ann's Wood Grid reference SW547372. 1.5 acres. This small area of woodland lies on the west bank of the Hayle Estuary, on the edge of Lelant village. Owned by the Woodland Trust, which plans to maintain it as a village amenity.

Antony Wood Grid reference SX401547. 0.33 acre. This small wood, at the village of Antony, has been planted recently and will be maintained on behalf of the village as a memorial to the late Lady Carew Pole. It is leased to the Woodland Trust.

Benskin's Wood Grid reference SX409539. 2.75 acres. Situated at St John, Torpoint, the wood offers views over Plymouth Sound and the River Tamar. It is only partly wooded and many of the trees have been planted recently. Owned by the Woodland Trust.

Lavethan Wood Grid reference SX104730. 25 acres. Not far from the village of Blisland, on the edge of Bodmin Moor and within the Bodmin Moor Area of Outstanding Natural Beauty. A broadleaved wood, dominated by oak and beech, lying in the valley of a tributary of the River Camel and offering riverside walks. Access is at the eastern end, from the road leading south from Blisland towards the A30. Owned by the Woodland Trust.

Shute Wood Grid reference SW742522. 0.5 acre. Situated at Trevellas, near St Agnes, half of this small wood is recent planting. Owned by the Woodland Trust.

CUMBRIA

Dufton Ghyll Wood Grid reference NY687250. 25 acres. Close to the village of Dufton near Appleby, on the western edge of the Pennines, just off the Pennine Way. Part of this wooded valley contains mature beech, oak and birch woodland. A large area was cleared some years ago, and has been replanted. A stream runs through the valley, and there are views of the Pennines. Access is by footpath, one of which leads from Dufton (at grid reference NY689250). The wood is owned by the Woodland Trust.

Round Hill Wood Grid reference SD526909. 1.5 acres. Although small, this wood on the edge of Kendal is an important feature of the landscape, and is protected by a tree preservation order. Owned by the Woodland Trust.

Scroggs Wood Grid reference SD512906. 3 acres. On the southern edge of Kendal, this wood is an amenity feature providing access to the bank of the River Kent. Owned by the Woodland Trust.

DERBYSHIRE

Burrs Wood Grid reference SK305755. 30 acres. The wood is situated near Chesterfield, in a quiet, steep valley on the edge of the Peak District National Park. Its unusual character derives from several rocky ridges and steep gullies. Containing a variety of tree and shrub species, it is mainly dominated by very old coppice oak, ash and sycamore, with an area of elm which so far has not been affected by Dutch elm disease. Other species include rowan, silver birch, yew, sallow and hazel. A small stream runs through the wood. Access is from the road running from the B6051 along the eastern side of the wood. A track leading from the road to the centre of the wood will eventually be extended to form a circular walk. The wood is owned by the Woodland Trust.

Ladybower Wood Grid reference SK205867. 40 acres. This wood, near Bamford, lies on millstone grit and is dominated by oak, with birch and rowan. It is a nature reserve owned and managed by the county trust for nature conservation, whose aim is to protect it from grazing sheep and to allow tree regeneration. There is a footpath across one corner of the wood but no open access; you need permission from the trust to enter the wood itself.

DEVON

Avon Valley Woods Grid reference SX736509 to SX732486. 100 acres. This is really two woods, called Woodleigh and Titcombe, with part of a third, Bedlime. They extend for almost 2 miles along the banks of the River Avon, in the South Hams north of Kingsbridge, within the South Devon Area of Outstanding Natural Beauty. A footpath runs beside the river for the entire length of the woods and a disused railway line from South Brent to Kingsbridge also runs beside them. Formerly the woods were managed as oak coppice, which was the system typical of this part of Devon. Although they are not being coppiced at present there are also areas of sweet-chestnut coppice, as well as many other tree and shrub species. Some areas are being actively converted to high forest. There are many flowering plants and mosses, the common dormouse (*Muscardinus avellanarius*) has been recorded there, and the river provides a habitat for otters. Owned by the Woodland Trust.

Axmouth-Lyme Regis Undercliffs Grid reference SY255898-333914. 790 acres. Situated on the undercliffs at Lyme Bay, between Lyme Regis and the mouth of the Axe, this is an area of considerable

176

geological interest. The woodland it supports is believed to have developed during this century, and trees have also been planted. The main species include beech, ash, holm and Turkey oak, silver fir, and pines. It is a National Nature Reserve. Admission, away from the coastal footpath which traverses the whole length of the reserve, is by permit, obtainable from the regional office of the Nature Conservancy Council.

Bailey Wood Grid reference SS521275. 1 acre. At Lovacott, near Bideford, this was recently planted and will mature as oak woodland. Owned by the Woodland Trust.

Bere Alston Copse
Bere Ferrers Copse Grid reference SX456670 and SX452639 respectively. 0.5 acre each. These two copses are of great visual importance, since they lie at the southern end of the high ridge of land between the Rivers Tamar and Tavy, in a region with few woods. One is at Bere Alston, the other at Bere Ferrers. Owned by the Woodland Trust.

Buck's and Keivell's Woods Grid reference SS357234. 33.75 acres. Situated in the North Devon Area of Outstanding Natural Beauty between Buck's Mills and Clovelly, Keivell's Wood lies in a valley running down to the sea and Buck's Wood along the adjacent clifftops. They are dominated by oak, suited to the exposed site. Formerly the oak was coppiced, but this is not being done at present. The North Devon Coast Path along the top of the cliffs passes through Buck's Wood. Access to the wood is easiest from Buck's Mills village. The woods are owned by the Woodland Trust.

Clayton Wood Grid reference SY068929. 2.5 acres. This is new woodland, planted in 1980, and situated within the East Devon Area of Outstanding Natural Beauty, at West Hill, to the west of Ottery St Mary. Owned by the Woodland Trust.

Cleaveland Wood Grid reference SX437651. 4.5 acres. Situated in the Tamar Valley, near Weir Quay, this wood has a long-abandoned mine chimney near its edge. Owned by the Woodland Trust.

Crowndale Wood Grid reference SX474733. 2.5 acres. Bounded on the west by the Tavistock Canal, and not far from Tavistock, access to this wood of mature trees is from the canal towpath. Owned by the Woodland Trust.

Dishcombe Wood Grid reference SX660933. 4.5 acres. Situated in the Dartmoor National Park, about 5 miles east of Okehampton, this wood began as an attractive line of hedgerow trees bordering a lane off the A30. In order to save the trees the adjacent field was bought and has been planted as mixed broadleaved woodland. Owned by the Woodland Trust.

Fordy Park Wood Grid reference SS818058. 1.75 acres. This small wood at Sandford, near Crediton, is an important landscape feature. Owned by the Woodland Trust.

Hardwick Wood Grid reference SX530555. 53 acres. Situated on the eastern edge of Plymouth, with views over Saltram House (owned by the National Trust) and Plymouth to the south, and Dartmoor to the north, this wood is an important feature of the landscape, and is easily recognised by the radio mast just outside its south-eastern boundary. It is an old estate plantation that has developed into high forest. Access is through a gate on the south-western edge (grid reference SX527554), adjacent to the road. There are many footpaths and rides. Five acres of the wood are leased by the Woodland Trust from the National Trust, the remainder is owned by the Woodland Trust.

Hemborough Beeches Grid reference SX828522. 1.75 acres. This wood consists of a group of beeches near Hemborough Post, close to the B3207 road from Modbury to Dartmouth. Owned by the Woodland Trust.

Hollacombe Woods and Quarry Grid reference SX527506. 16.5 acres. A long-abandoned quarry surrounded by woodland containing a wide range of broadleaved species, supporting a rich wildlife. It forms a wild, attractive area which had not been open to the public before it was acquired by the Woodland Trust.

Littlewood Grid reference SX539684. 1 acre. This wood, in the village of Dousland in the Dartmoor National Park, is of visual importance, and is owned by the Woodland Trust.

Liverton Copse Grid reference SY025823. 7 acres. Lying in the centre of Exmouth, this copse was formerly planted with conifers, which were felled except for a shelter belt on the seaward side. The area has now been replanted with oak, ash and lime under a Create a Wood Scheme. Owned by the Woodland Trust.

178

Longstone Wood Grid reference SX467753. 2.5 acres. A prominent landmark on the north side of the A384 Tavistock to Launceston road, not far from Tavistock. The wood is dominated by mature beech and ash. Owned by the Woodland Trust, but not open to the public.

Martyn's Wood Grid reference SS336031. 2 acres. This wood, near Holsworthy, consists of a hedge with tall trees adjacent to a field of bracken and brambles, and a valuable wildlife habitat. Owned by the Woodland Trust.

Netherhaddon Spinney Grid reference SY253975. 0.25 acre. This tiny wood lies within the East Devon Area of Outstanding Natural Beauty, in the village of Shute, near Axminster. Owned by the Woodland Trust.

Northdown Wood Grid reference SS923062. 22.5 acres. Before its purchase by the Woodland Trust, this wood had been in the ownership of the same family for more than 150 years. It comprises mixed woodland with a rich understorey and will be managed as a nature reserve. Access is from a path leading from the A3072 near Thorverton.

Page Wood Grid reference SY137879. 1 acre. Situated on the western side of Salcombe Hill, at Salcome Regis, near Sidmouth, this wood is clearly visible from Sidmouth. Owned by the Woodland Trust.

The Pinetum Grid reference SY317934. 7 acres. Situated in the East Devon Area of Outstanding Natural Beauty, near Uplyme, to the north of Lyme Regis, this wood is partly dominated by oak and beech and is partly an arboretum growing specimen conifers. These are thought to include Britain's tallest Prince Albert's yew (*Saxegotha conspicua*) and Japanese red cedar (*Cryptomeria japonica*). There are also fine specimens of Caucasian fir (*Abies nordmanniana*), and Wellingtonia (*Sequoiadendron giganteum*), with newly planted conifers filling gaps left by wind-blown trees. The wood is within the East Devon Area of Outstanding Natural Beauty, and is owned by the Woodland Trust.

The Plantation Grid reference SX734385. 2 acres. This mature, mixed broadleaved wood, in the South Devon Area of Outstanding Natural Beauty, lies behind Salcombe, to which it provides a background when seen from the estuary. Owned by the Woodland Trust.

Point and Whitehall Woods Grid reference SX483879. 23.5 acres. Situated at Combebow, near Bridestowe, beside the A30 road between Launceston and Okehampton, this is an important area of wildlife habitat woodland. Owned by the Woodland Trust, but not open to the public.

Rectory Field Grid reference SX842696. 5.5 acres. An area of woodland-pasture, at East Ogwell, the field formerly contained two groups of trees together with mature trees in the surrounding hedgerows. Two more groups of trees have been added. The field is owned by the Woodland Trust, and is grazed.

Shaptor and Furzeleigh Woods Grid reference SX818794 to SX804815. 195 acres. Most of these woods lie inside Dartmoor National Park, in the Wray Valley which links Bovey Tracey and Mortonhampstead, one of the most beautiful wooded valleys in Devon. The woods contain beech, oak and hazel. Part of the woodland is being actively managed as coppice-with-standards of hazel, beneath a canopy of oak. The woods support many species of birds, including wood warblers (*Phylloscopus sibilatrix*) and tree pipits (*Anthus trivialis*). From Shaptor Rock there are splendid views of the surrounding moorland and countryside. As there are several disused mine shafts within the woods, you are advised to keep to the footpaths. The woods are owned by the Woodland Trust. Access is by footpaths which leave the road at grid references SX818794 and SX819797, or by a footpath which leaves the road near Slade Cross (grid reference SX800813), enters the wood at SX805809, leaves the wood at SX809808, and rejoins the road near Bottor Rock (SX818804). Conservation volunteers have made a path through the woods.

Shears Copse Grid reference SS614097. 2.75 acres. Situated on the edge of Winkleigh Aerodrome, this copse comprises scrub woodland that has regenerated naturally from coppice. It is noted for its plentiful and varied bird life. Owned by the Woodland Trust.

Snakey Copse Grid reference SX874675. 1 acre. Situated near Kingskerswell, this wood has a perimeter footpath, popular locally. Owned by the Woodland Trust.

South Plantation Grid reference ST114094. 30 acres. Situated at Sheldon, near Honiton, this wood contains a mixture of broadleaves and conifers in an area with much coniferous forest. When the conifers are economically mature they will be felled and replaced by broadleaved species. The wood is owned by the Woodland Trust.

Wedd's Copse
Tanglewood Grid reference SX484745. 3 acres. Wedd's Copse lies on former railway land, adjacent to Tanglewood, which occupies a disused quarry. Near Tavistock, they are owned by the Woodland Trust and are not open to the public.

Westcott Wood Grid reference SX785873. 14 acres. In the valley of a small tributary of the River Teign, near Doccombe in the Dartmoor National Park. This conifer wood will eventually be felled and the area replanted with broadleaved species. Owned by the Woodland Trust.

Whitleigh Wood Grid reference SX482599. 38.25 acres. A gift to the Woodland Trust from the City of Plymouth. This mixed broadleaved wood contains oak, ash, birch, and sycamore. Rubbish has been tipped there, but management plans include its clearance, with the help of local people. The wood is very popular locally, and access is provided partly by land that has been cleared to form a glade along the route of a water main. The wood lies on the western side of the B3373 road just north of Crownhill, and access is from the road.

Wistman's Wood Grid reference SX612772. 10 acres. This area of oak woodland on the west-facing side of the Dart Valley, Dartmoor, lies on granite and unlike many Dartmoor woodlands is dominated by pedunculate oak rather than sessile oak. There is also some rowan, hazel, holly and willow, and the epiphytic flora is luxuriant, lichens being especially well represented. The ground flora is rich in ferns. It is a Forest Nature Reserve owned by the Duchy of Cornwall and managed by the Nature Conservancy Council.

Woodcot Wood Grid reference SX734384. 7 acres. This wood occupies a prominent position on the western side of the Salcombe estuary, near Salcombe, within the South Devon Area of Outstanding Natural Beauty. It is leased by the Woodland Trust.

Yarner Wood Grid reference SX785788. 370 acres. This wood lies

181

along the valleys of the Yarner and Woodstock streams and covers the spur of land between them. There is a difference of more than 700ft between the lowest and highest points. The canopy is mainly of sessile oak, some of the trees being large, with an understorey of rowan and holly. There is also birch, as well as plantations of conifers and hardwoods. The wood forms part of a National Nature Reserve. Visitors are welcome but are asked to keep to the marked paths. You will need a permit to carry out research, obtainable from the regional office of the Nature Conservancy Council.

Yeo Copse Grid reference SS801151. 8 acres. This attractive area of oak trees lies on the south side of the Sturcombe River valley. There is an old mill leat close to the public footpath at the bottom of the wood. The wood is owned by the Woodland Trust.

DORSET

Boyden Wood Grid reference ST404026. 2 acres. This recently planted wood was formerly a field. It lies within the Dorset Area of Outstanding Natural Beauty, at Blackdown, near Beaminster, and is owned by the Woodland Trust.

Brounlie Wood Grid reference ST601118. 3.75 acres. Situated at Beer Hackett, near Sherborne. A mixed wood, planted recently, owned by the Woodland Trust.

Charlton Beeches Grid reference ST897041. 3 acres. When new houses were built at Charlton Marshall this beech wood was retained as an amenity feature. Owned by the Woodland Trust.

Eileen Fraser Beeches Grid reference ST616206. 0.1 acre. This is a narrow strip of land bordering a secondary road leading from Sandford Orcas which has been planted with a line of beech trees. It is owned by the Woodland Trust.

Fifehead Wood Grid reference ST775215. 50 acres. This wood is situated near the village of Fifehead Magdalen, not far from Stour Hill on the A30 road near West Stour. Part of it lies on a low hill, and part on a river floodplain. There is a drainage system on the lower, western part of the wood, but the system is derelict and the land is very wet, and ecologically important for that reason. The higher eastern end of the wood is much drier. Part of the wood is oak high forest, but much of it used to be managed as coppice-with-standards, with hazel under a canopy of oak and ash. Coppicing has been reintroduced in some areas which are now being worked actively and the high forest is also being thinned. Part of the wood was once an osier bed, but now contains oak, ash, and plants tolerant of the marshy conditions. Access is from the village of Fifehead Magdalen, or from the road at the eastern end of the wood (grid reference ST778218), where cars may be parked. A public footpath crosses the wood and passes through surrounding meadows, and there is a good network of rides. The wood is owned by the Woodland Trust.

Folke Wood Grid reference ST657135. 1.25 acres. This is an old orchard bordering a road which has been planted with a mixture of broadleaved trees. Owned by the Woodland Trust, but not open to the public.

Furzehill Grid reference SU012018. 2 acres. About thirty years ago this small field at Colehill, near Wimborne Minster, was planted with clumps of trees, some native, some exotic. Oak has regenerated naturally within the clumps, and more clumps are to be planted. Owned by the Woodland Trust but not open to the public.

Horse Close Wood Grid reference ST715045. 41 acres. Lying under the steep slopes of Church Hill, at Alton Pancras, not far from the Cerne Abbas giant and within the Dorset Area of Outstanding Natural Beauty, this wood is almost certainly ancient. It contains oak, ash, alder and hazel coppice, as well as large trees, most of them oak. It used to be managed as coppice-with-standards, with oak over hazel, and coppicing has been reintroduced with the help of the Dorset Conservation Corps. There are no rights of way through the wood, but there is an access route for visitors (grid reference ST718046). Owned by the Woodland Trust.

Stonecrop Wood Grid reference SY988955. 2 acres. A small mixed wood at Broadstone, owned by the Woodland Trust.

DURHAM

Hawthorn Dene Grid reference NZ433457. 165 acres. Despite its name, which is derived from nearby Hawthorn village, this wood is not dominated by hawthorn, although hawthorn is invading some areas that were formerly cleared for agriculture and then abandoned. It is a nature reserve managed by the county trust for nature conservation. The village is about 1.5 miles north of Easington on the B1432 and north of the village there is a minor road leading east towards a signposted quarry. A gate gives access to the reserve by which cars should normally be parked – without causing obstruction. (If vehicular access into the reserve is required for any special purpose, arrangements to obtain a key should be made by contacting the Durham County Conservation Office, Durham 69797, or Mr James at Keeper's Cottage, nearby.)

Pontburn Woods Grid reference NZ147562. 60 acres. Situated in the Derwent Valley, near Consett, west of Newcastle-upon-Tyne, these are among the most important and largest broadleaved woodlands in the area. They are accessible from the B6310 road, where there is parking, and from the Derwent Valley Walkway, which crosses the woods by the Hamsterley Viaduct. The woods are owned by the Woodland Trust.

Witton-le-Wear Grid reference NZ161313. 84 acres. This area of mature alder woodland is a nature reserve owned and managed by the county trust for nature conservation, and includes an area recently afforested. It is at Low Barns, east of Witton-le-Wear, and the entrance is clearly marked. Parking. Access is confined to the nature trail.

DYFED

Coed Allt Troed-y-rhiw-fawr Grid reference SN413255. 39 acres. Standing at the entrance to the wooded gorge of the Afon Gwili, near Bronwydd 5 miles from Carmarthen, the wood dominates the view from the south, rising almost vertically from the river to the top of the valley. It contains a wide variety of tree and shrub species, the commonest being ash and oak, with smaller amounts of birch, cherry and sycamore. Access is by a track passing by Troed-y-rhiw Farm from the B4301 road, a mile from its junction with the A484 at Bronwydd Arms. There is room for roadside parking close to the entrance to the track. Owned by the Woodland Trust.

Coed Rheidol Grid reference SN7478. 115 acres. This reserve comprises mainly sessile oak woodland, on the sides of the Rheidol valley. It is influenced strongly by the River Rheidol and its tributaries, which have cut steep-sided ravines through Silurian sediments. Birch is dominant locally, and there is also ash, wych-elm and hazel. In the Allt Ddu section of the reserve some of the oaks have been managed in the past by coppicing. Subsequent growth-rates are being studied from the cut stumps, some of which are more than 100 years old. In other parts of the reserve a programme of thinning is being undertaken, to diversify the even-aged canopy and to encourage natural regeneration. A permit is required to enter this National Nature Reserve, obtainable from the regional office of the Nature Conservancy Council, but public access is permitted to parts of the valley via a nature trail at Devil's Bridge.

Coed Tyddyn du Grid reference SN272426. 47 acres. Situated on a tributary of the Teifi Valley, near Cenarth and not far from Cardigan, the wood consists of a small area which is probably ancient and a larger area which has resulted from natural colonisation following the abandonment of farming in the area about a century ago. Ash will come to dominate the wood unless its regeneration is reduced by management. It is now the largest area of broadleaved, lowland woodland in the Ceredigon district, and is a Site of Special Scientific Interest. Access is by a lane running through Tyddyn du Farm from a small road about halfway between the A484 and B4570 roads. Most of the wood is owned by the Woodland Trust, but not the unwooded central area.

Tregeyb Wood Grid reference SN641217. 70 acres. This wood, lying inside the Brecon Beacons National Park, is a Site of Special Scientific Interest and an important landscape feature. When it was owned commercially a large area was felled, but felling has ceased and a 4 acre field inside the area will be allowed to regenerate naturally. There is ample roadside parking and the wood is well provided with access rides. Owned by the Woodland Trust.

ESSEX

Blakes Wood Grid reference TL775064. 104 acres. This area of mixed deciduous woodland at Little Baddow is dominated by hornbeam and sweet chestnut, but also includes oak, birch and other species, and is rich in herbs and birds. Scrub is being cleared and coppicing reinstated, which is improving the habitat for insects. It is a nature reserve, managed by Essex Naturalists' Trust on behalf of the National Trust. Access is from Riffhams Chase, which extends from the western end of Danbury village to Little Baddow. Parking just inside the reserve.

185

Copperas Wood Grid reference TL200313. 34 acres. This area of mixed deciduous woodland, near the shore of the Stour estuary about a mile north-west of Ramsey, contains coppiced sweet chestnut with oak standards, and there is also some small-leaved lime. It is a nature reserve managed by Essex Naturalists' Trust. Access is by a track leading north from the Manningtree to Ramsey road (B1352).

Stour Wood Grid reference TH190315. 134 acres. Situated beside the B1352 road between Wrabness and Ramsey, not far from Harwich, this is an ancient woodland, a Site of Special Scientific Interest, and forms part of an internationally important reserve managed by the Royal Society for the Protection of Birds. Until recently it was managed as a pure sweet-chestnut coppice-with-standards wood, and there are plans to reintroduce coppicing. It is one of the most important conservation woods in Essex. It contains 14 species of mammal, 40 species of breeding birds, and 18 types of trees, including wild service, as well as an unrecorded number of species of flowering plants and invertebrate animals. Wildlife is being encouraged by replacing some of the sweet chestnut with other species. There are two public footpaths through the wood, several rides, and views across the Stour estuary – the Stour made famous by the paintings of Constable. The wood is owned by the Woodland Trust.

GLOUCESTERSHIRE

Bigsweir Wood Grid reference SO544056. 110 acres. Lying within the Wye Valley Area of Outstanding Natural Beauty, and a Grade II Site of Special Scientific Interest, this wood contains large areas of oak, as well as beech and lime coppice. It used to be managed as coppice-with-standards, the beech and lime being coppiced beneath oak. There are plans to reintroduce coppicing. Elsewhere the area is high forest dominated by oak. Offa's Dyke, and the Offa's Dyke Long-Distance Footpath run through the wood, which is situated beside the A466 Monmouth to Chepstow road, near Redbrook; access at the southern end, from a small road which leaves the main road at Bigsweir Bridge. The wood is owned by the Woodland Trust.

Cotswold Commons and Beechwoods Grid reference SO894131-9011. Approximately 800 acres. This is an area of beech woodland containing high forest, some of which is 300 years old, though most is about 150 years old. In addition to the beech there is some ash and understorey holly and yew. It is a National Nature Reserve. No permit is required to visit the area unless you wish to walk away from the public footpaths and bridleways.

Frith Wood Grid reference SO875085. 54 acres. This area of mature beech woodland lies on a ridge between the Slad and Painswick valleys, forming a dense stand of trees probably planted in the last century. The trees are tall and straight, and there is excellent natural regeneration. It is a nature reserve managed by the county trust for nature conservation, is open to the public, and is well served by miles of tracks. Visitors must keep to the tracks; blue arrows mark the bridle paths for riders. Access is from Bulls Cross, beside the Slad Valley road (B4070), and cars should be parked at Bulls Cross and not inside the reserve.

Parish and Oldhills Woods Grid reference SO906027. 35 acres. These two woods lie in the 'Golden Valley' beside the River Frome, within the Cotswolds Area of Outstanding Natural Beauty, at Chalford, near Stroud. They consist largely of beech high forest, with a number of other native species, and are being thinned, mainly to remove many dead elms. Footpaths run through the wood, and access is from a narrow road through Chalford. The woods are owned by the Woodland Trust.

Stanley Wood Grid reference SO895015 to SO817022. 93 acres. Lying in the Cotswold Area of Outstanding Natural Beauty, near Stroud, the wood stretches for 1.5 miles along the scarp slope of the Cotswolds above the villages of Kings Stanley and Leonard Stanley and is part of the impressive western edge of the Cotswolds, visible from much of the Severn Valley. It was felled in the 1960s and parts were replanted with conifers, but there has been considerable regeneration of ash and beech and the wood is being thinned to promote the broadleaved trees and help the rich ground flora which is typical of an ancient woodland on limestone. The Cotswold Way long-distance path runs through the wood. Coaley Park Picnic Site, with car parking, is at the western end. The wood has many public footpaths. Access is from the B4066 Stroud to Fursley road. Owned by the Woodland Trust.

'This England' Wood Grid reference SO875083. 5 acres. Lying within the Cotswold Area of Outstanding Natural Beauty, at Slad, this recently planted field belongs to the Woodland Trust.

GRAMPIAN

Dinnet Oakwood Grid reference NO464980. 49 acres. An area of oak woodland, containing both pedunculate and sessile oaks, some of them more than 100 years old; it is one of the few examples of oakwood in the eastern Highlands. Though probably planted, it resembles semi-natural upland oakwood. In addition to the oaks it contains birch, rowan, hazel, ash, aspen and alder. A National Nature Reserve.

Morrone Birkwoods Grid reference NO1390. 247 acres. This area of downy-birch woodland, on the Dalradian calcareous schist above Braemar, is the best British example of a subalpine birch-juniper wood on a basic soil. The understorey is of juniper, which gives protection from grazing to many montane herbs. A National Nature Reserve.

GWENT

Cwm Clydach Grid reference SO2112. 50 acres. This area comprises two woodland blocks (Coed Fedw-ddu and Coed Ffyddlwn) located on the southern side of the Afon Clydach ravine. The underlying millstone grit and Carboniferous limestone give rise to a range of acidic and base-rich soils. The woods consist mainly of a mature, self-regenerating beech, which is here at the western limit of its natural range. There are some areas of mixed woodland (ash, elm, lime, field maple, oak and whitebeam) on the flushed lower slopes, with a rich ground flora; and there are small areas of beech-dominated woodland over a poor ground flora with species characteristic of acid soils, such as bilberry, heath bedstraw and wavy-hair grass. These woods are a National Nature Reserve. A permit to enter is obtainable from the regional officer of the Nature Conservancy Council.

GWYNEDD

Coed Allt Grid reference SH620357. 8 acres. Situated at Talsarnau, near Harlech, within the Snowdonia National Park. A young oak woodland which has developed naturally on a very steep slope after fences excluded grazing sheep. Ravens nest in the crags. The slope is very steep and the ground surface unstable – you are not advised to enter. Owned by the Woodland Trust.

Coed Avens Grid reference SH476923. 1.65 acres. This field, at Amlwch, Anglesey, was planted in 1983 with broadleaved trees. A public footpath runs through it. Owned by the Woodland Trust.

188

Coed Cymerau Isaf Grid reference SH691425. 79.74 acres. The wood lies at the head of the Vale of Ffestiniog, one of the most important woodland valleys in Snowdonia, and inside the Snowdonia National Park. It consists mainly of oak woodland but there are several areas of open pasture and marshy land which are remnants of a small agricultural holding that was abandoned some years ago. The topography is made up of rocky knolls and small dells affording occasional glimpses into the Vale. Two public footpaths around the wood offer a gentle circular walk that includes most of it. Access is through a green gate beside the A496 Blaenau Ffestiniog to Maentwrog road, and there is a large layby where cars can be parked. Owned by the Woodland Trust.

Coed Dolgarrog Grid reference SH7666. 170 acres. This area of mainly oak woodland, containing both species of oak as well as hybrids, extends along the steep western side of the Dyffryn Conwy and is bounded at both ends by steep ravines. It ranges in altitude from 100 to 1,000ft, but is sheltered by the valley sides. In the south the wood extends up the valley of the Afon Ddu, and there it contains the Ardda Alderwood, at an altitude of 690 to 850ft. At one time such woods were common, but many were enclosed in the sixteenth century. The area is leased by the Nature Conservancy Council as a National Nature Reserve. You will need a permit to enter it, obtainable from the regional office of the Nature Conservancy Council.

Coed Llechwedd Grid reference SH595320. 61 acres. Lying within the Snowdonia National Park, and a Grade II Site of Special Scientific Interest, this upland wood is regenerating since sheep were excluded. It lies on the steep slopes of what used to be a sea cliff. In the thirteenth century, when Harlech Castle was built, the sea came to the foot of the cliff, and ships moored below the castle. A sand and shingle spit developed, and now the Castle and the wood are landlocked. Access is from two public footpaths leading from the B4573 road about 1.5 miles from Harlech. Owned by the Woodland Trust.

Coed Lletywalter Grid reference SH600275. 94 acres. This attractive oak woodland contains many wildlife habitats, ranging from marshy areas near a lake within the wood to rocky outcrops in the north-western corner; and it is rich in mosses and ferns. It is a Grade II Site of Special Scientific Interest, and may become a National Nature Reserve. The wood also contains remnants of former mining activity. It is situated within the Snowdonia National Park, at Llanbedr 3 miles south of Harlech. Access is from a minor road which leaves the A496 at Llanbedr, and several public footpaths lead from the edges of the wood. There are fine views towards the western slopes of the Rhinog mountains. Owned by the Woodland Trust.

Coed Tyddyn Badyn Grid reference SH565669. 7.5 acres. This wood, at Bangor, was replanted with conifers some years ago, but some alder, birch, and willow survived and is growing vigorously. In time a broadleaved wood will be re-established. Owned by the Woodland Trust.

Coed y Rhygen Grid reference SM6836. 67 acres. This wood lies on the western side of Trawsfynydd Lake, 650 to 1,500ft above sea level, and has an annual rainfall of nearly 80in. The land is very broken. Sessile oak and birch are the most common trees, usually with large old oaks growing among birch, but at the eastern end of the wood birch is dominant, probably because the oak was removed at some time in the past. There is also some rowan and willow. Part of the wood is believed to be ancient. It is a National Nature Reserve. A permit to enter must be obtained from the regional office of the Nature Conservancy Council, from whom an information leaflet is available.

HAMPSHIRE

Selborne Hanger Grid reference SU735337. Made famous by Gilbert White in his *Natural History of Selborne*, this area of beech woodland is owned by the National Trust, together with several other parts of Selborne Hill.

HEREFORD AND WORCESTER

Chaddesley-Randan Woods Grid reference SO914736. 252 acres. A part of the former Feckenham Forest, these woods consist almost entirely of mature oak high forest, with both species of oak present, together with a mixture of other species, including hazel, ash, alder and birch, some of which has been coppiced in the past. They are a National Nature Reserve. There are adequate public and courtesy paths; no permit to visit is needed.

Nupend Wood Grid reference SO580354. 12 acres. This area of woodland near Fownhope lies on a ridge dominated on one side by yew and on the other by coppiced oak, field maple, ash, beech and some wild service trees. There are many lime-loving flowers and a rich animal life. It is a nature reserve owned and managed by the county trust for nature conservation. There is parking at the entrance to the reserve beside the Fownhope to Woolhope road, from where a path leads along the side of the wood to some rough stone steps which give access to the reserve.

Pepper Wood Grid reference SO937747. 134 acres. A remnant of Feckenham Forest, this wood was once managed as coppice-with-standards of mixed species. Much of the remainder is managed high forest. It is now cared for by local volunteers who run it as a community woodland. Coppicing has been reintroduced to enhance its wildlife value and to provide wood products. Oak and birch are the main trees, but many other species are present, including wild service and alder buckthorn. The wood lies 3 miles north-west of Bromsgrove. Access is from the southern side of the wood; car park at grid reference SO938744. Owned by the Woodland Trust.

Wassell Wood Grid reference SO795775. 54.5 acres. Standing on a prominent hill overlooking the Severn Valley, 2 miles west of Kidderminster, much of this area of mature oak woodland was felled, despite a tree-preservation order. It is now being replanted by the Woodland Trust. Access is from a minor road along the western boundary of the wood, reached by taking the B4190 towards Wolverley from the Kidderminster to Bewdley road, then taking the first turn on the left into Trimpley Lane. Owned by the Woodland Trust.

Woodland at Symonds Yat West Grid reference SO557158. 14 acres. Situated within the Lower Wye Valley Area of Outstanding Natural Beauty, and a Grade I Site of Special Scientific Interest, this broadleaved wood is clearly visible from Symonds Yat Rock, and forms an important feature of the valley landscape. It includes several derelict mineshafts which provide interesting habitats for wildlife – but you are advised to keep to the footpaths – and is of major conservation importance. Owned by the Woodland Trust.

Wyre Forest Grid reference SO759766. Approximately 600 acres. The forest lies on the boundary between Hereford–Worcester and Shropshire, to the west of the River Severn. It consists predominantly of sessile oakwood, mainly of coppice origin, but mixed deciduous woodland has developed in the valleys, with wild service, ash, elm, small-leaved lime and alder. The field layer is diverse, varying according to the soil type; and the forest is rich in fungi, bryophytes and lichens. The fauna is very rich. The forest is a National Nature Reserve but no permit is needed to visit it.

HERTFORDSHIRE

Fox Covert
Fordhams Wood Grid reference TL334397 (Fox Covert), TL335395 (Fordhams Wood). 30.5 acres. These woods lie at the edge of Therfield Heath, near Royston, and both are dominated by beech. Fox Covert is mature, with a flora typical of chalk woodland, but has suffered badly from beech bark disease, and felling and replanting may be necessary in the long term. Fordhams Wood contains areas of elm, ash and sycamore in addition to beech. Each wood is a nature reserve managed by the county trust for nature conservation. Access is from a footpath leading from the west side of Therfield Road, immediately to the south of Royston golf course and not far from the junction with the A505.

Hoddesdonpark Wood Grid reference TL348088. 150 acres. Ermine Street runs along the western boundary of this largely mature oak high forest, and the wood is bordered by a number of pollarded hornbeams. It falls within the same Grade I Site of Special Scientific Interest as Wormley Wood (see below). There are many footpaths and rides, and access is from Ermine Street Roman road at the western boundary and Lord Street along the northern boundary. Owned by the Woodland Trust.

Wormley Wood Grid reference TL320060. 340 acres. A Grade I Site of Special Scientific Interest, this is the largest and most important oak and hornbeam high forest remaining largely in its semi-natural state. Almost all of the wood is ancient, and its interest lies more in the structure of the woodland itself than in its ground flora, although there is a unique range of mosses, and an interesting system of streams. Part of the wood was clear-felled and planted with conifers in the 1970s, and this area is being restored to deciduous woodland. Situated close to Hertford, access is from White Stubbs Lane at the northern end of the wood. There are many paths and rides through the wood. Owned by the Woodland Trust.

HIGHLAND

Ariundle Wood Grid reference NM8464. 296 acres. This area of sessile oak woodland lies on a slope above the Strontian River. The trees are 40 to 150 years old and most were formerly coppiced, forming a fairly pure stand, but with some wych-elm, ash and hazel. The wood is important for its bryophytes and lichens. It is part of the Loch Sunart Woodlands National Nature Reserve. Access is by the old mining track from Ariundle, north of Strontian.

Beinn Eighe Grid reference NH0046. 321 acres. The mature Scots pine woodland beside Loch Maree used to be one of the finest in Scotland, but it suffered badly from timber extraction during the two World Wars and now the tree cover is very variable. There are areas of continuous woodland, but much of it consists of rather open pine heath. The dense pine wood occurs in the west, the pine occurring with holly, rowan, ivy and some oak. On more calcareous soils the pine gives way to downy-birch woodland. Bryophytes and lichens grow abundantly throughout the area, which lies within a National Nature Reserve. The wood can be seen from a nature trail which is open to the public throughout the year. Beinn Eighe National Nature Reserve also includes a mountain area above the woods and covers more than 18 square miles in total. It is the oldest National Nature Reserve in Britain and has been declared a habitat of international importance under the United Nations Man and Biosphere Programme. The importance of the reserve lies in its rock formations, its wildlife, and its Highland pine forest growing along the shores of the loch. In 1983, the Nature Conservancy Council was awarded a Council of Europe Diploma for its management of the Beinn Eighe reserve.

Glen Affric Grid reference NH2424. 4,942 acres. This area of native Scots pine and birch woodland stretches mainly along the south side of Glen Affric from the head of Strathglass to the western end of Loch Affric. Juniper occurs locally and rowan is common in the birch areas, mainly in the east, and there is alder and willow along the streams. It is owned by the Forestry Commission, which has undertaken replanting and encouraged regeneration to restore the pine woods.

Glencripesdale Woods Grid reference NM6861. 230 acres. These woods lie on the slopes south of Loch Sunart, in very shady, humid conditions. They consist mainly of ash and hazel on rich calcareous soils. The woods are important also for their bryophytes and they form part of the Loch Sunart Woodlands National Nature Reserve. A permit to enter them is obtainable from the regional office of the Nature Conservancy Council.

Inverpolly Woods Grid reference NC1013. 778 acres. This area contains twenty or so separate and scattered birchwoods, ranging in altitude from sea level to 900ft, and ranging widely in size, the best being in the north-west, in Gleann an Strathain and on the south side of the Kirkaig River. The woods are dominated by downy birch, with rowan, hazel, alder, occasional bird-cherry and eared sallow (*Salix aurita*) which is plentiful, especially on wetter ground. The area is a National Nature Reserve.

Mound Alderwoods Grid reference NH7698. 650 acres. This area of alder and willow woodland in Sutherland has grown on an embankment (the Mound) built in the last century across the head of Loch Fleet to seal off part of the estuary. There are a few ridges, which probably projected above the water before the Mound was built, supporting Scots pine, and there are areas of swamp. It is a National Nature Reserve. A permit to enter is obtainable from the regional office of the Nature Conservancy Council.

Rassal Ashwood Grid reference NG8443. 210 acres. This is the most northerly area of true ash woodland in Britain, growing on Durness Limestone. The trees are widely spaced and some of them are large. The wood contains much hazel, a little downy birch, goat willow and rowan, and some hawthorn and blackthorn scrub; the lichen flora is of particular interest. A National Nature Reserve.

HUNTINGDONSHIRE

Holme Fen Grid reference TL2189. 640 acres. At one time this area was a bog associated with a large mere. It was drained for agriculture, then abandoned, and extensive birchwoods, of both silver and downy birch, have developed so that now Holme Fen is considered to be the finest wood of its type in lowland Britain. The birch stands are remarkably pure, although there is some oak, alder, willow and pine. It is a National Nature Reserve. A permit to enter it is obtainable from the regional office of the Nature Conservancy Council.

KENT

Blean Woods Grid reference TR118611. Complex totalling 7,060 acres, including a 2,000 acre National Nature Reserve, Clowes Wood of 1,500 acres, West Blean 3,000 acres, and East Blean, Ellenden and others amounting to 500 acres. These woods form part of the most extensive area of nearly continuous woodland on the London Clay, and the woods themselves are typical of the overall area. For many years they were managed as coppice-with-standards, sessile oak being the dominant standard, but there is also sessile oak coppice mixed with beech to the west, and beech dominates a small area of open high forest at the centre. In the north there is hornbeam coppice, and sweet-chestnut coppice in the south-central and south-eastern parts. Rowan is widespread and there is also wild service, alder and aspen. The ground flora is rich and the area is famous among entomologists. The woods are a National Nature Reserve. A permit to enter them is obtainable from the regional office of the Nature Conservancy Council.

Denge Wood Grid reference TR105525. 64 acres. This wood, situated at Garlinge Green in the Kent Downs Area of Outstanding Natural Beauty, is almost certainly ancient and the wide range of flowering plants suggests the wood has never been cleared. It contains hornbeam and sweet chestnut in separate areas, both still managed actively as coppice-with-standards, and many other tree species, including a fine stand of mature yew. There is a 14 acre area of chalk grassland in the centre of the wood which is rich in plant and insect species, and is of considerable conservation importance. Access is from the eastern side, by a minor road leading from Garlinge Green. Owned by the Woodland Trust.

Earley Wood Grid reference TR122504. 38 acres. This wood is situated near Petham in the Kent Downs Area of Outstanding Natural Beauty. It is coppice-with-standards, with mixed species; active coppicing was reintroduced during the early 1970s. Small areas of hazel, hornbeam and sweet-chestnut coppice are sold standing each year to a local merchant. An avenue of beeches runs through the centre of the wood and in spring there are many bluebells. The wood also contains orchids. The western half of the wood may be ancient and is separated from the eastern half by a bank and ditch. Access is easiest from the Waltham to Petham road on the western side. Owned by the Woodland Trust.

195

Flatroper's Wood Grid reference TQ862229. 87 acres. This area of mainly deciduous woodland growing on Tunbridge Wells sand, near Beckley, is dominated by oak with birch and sweet-chestnut coppice, and some alder and sallow along stream banks. There is a rich ground flora and many species of insects and birds are present. It is a nature reserve managed by the county trust for nature conservation. Access is along the western side of the reserve, from the Rye-Hawkhurst road (A268); parking at the entrances.

Ham Street Woods Grid reference TR004337. 239 acres. A compact coppice-with-standards woodland within the Orlestone and Ham Street Woods complex. The principal standard tree species is oak, with a variable mixture of birch and other minor species. Although there are local stands with coppice of oak, sweet chestnut or hazel, the most widespread species is hornbeam. Near stream-sides, stands also contain coppice of alder, ash and sallow. The presence of scattered wild service, gean, aspen and Midland hawthorn, together with elements of the ground flora, suggests that these are primary woodlands. Present management by the Nature Conservancy Council perpetuates coppice-with-standards in parts of the wood, but in other parts the coppice is being converted into a false high forest. Certain small areas receive special treatments aimed at the conservation of the rich insect fauna for which the complex is renowned. The varying treatments strongly influence the ground flora and associated fauna. The woods are a National Nature Reserve and, except on public rights of way, access requires a permit from the South-East Regional Office of the Nature Conservancy Council.

Hurst Wood Grid reference TQ568405. 42.25 acres. This wood lies in a small valley on the north-western edge of Tunbridge Wells. It appears on the first edition of the Ordnance Survey 1in map (1801) and its shape and size have changed little since then, although most of its mature timber has been cleared in the last forty years. Birch, oak, beech and willow have regenerated naturally, and a small area of larch was planted in 1963 by its former owners, the Forestry Commission, from whom it was purchased by the Woodland Trust. In time, natural regeneration or planting will change the open areas into woodland once more. A footpath runs through the wood and access is by public footpaths approaching from the north and south.

Park Wood Grid reference TR043527. 55 acres. This wood, situated near Chilham, in the Kent Downs Area of Outstanding Natural

Beauty, forms the most northerly part of Challock Forest. Much of the Forest has been planted with conifers, but Park Wood is said to be one of the best areas of deciduous woodland in East Kent because of the large number of plant and animal species it supports. It is a Site of Special Scientific Interest. The wood contains hazel, hornbeam and sweet-chestnut coppice, and yew and many other tree species, as well as shrubs and plants typical of a chalk soil. The coppice-with-standards system of management in the past contributed much to the present-day conservation value of the wood, and has been reintroduced over about two-thirds of it, sweet chestnut and hazel being coppiced in separate areas. Access is from the A252 road, where there is ample parking. Except for the north-eastern part, the wood is owned by the Woodland Trust.

LINCOLNSHIRE

Hatton Wood Grid reference TF1674. 86 acres. The eastern part of this wood consists of high forest dominated by lime and oak over a sparse shrub layer of hazel, with secondary oak-ash woodland at the eastern end and beside a stream in the north, and there is a small area of oak standards over hazel coppice. The wood forms part of Bardney Forest, which is owned by the Forestry Commission.

Kew Wood Grid reference TF412787. 1 acre. This small field has been planted recently. Owned by the Woodland Trust, it is not open to the public, but is visible from the road, at Aby, near Alford.

Nettleton Wood Grid reference TF098994. 25 acres. Lying just below the edge of the Lincolnshire Wolds, near Caistor, this area is partly wooded and partly new planting of ash, hazel, small-leaved lime, field maple and other species which eventually will be managed as coppice woodland. It will provide information on the rate of growth and productivity of this type of woodland, as well as data on the changing ecology of the planted area. Owned by the Woodland Trust.

Yalta Woods Grid reference TF320910. 6 acres. This small wood, near Fotherby, was planted with a variety of tree species by its former owner. A valuable addition to the North Lincolnshire landscape, which has few small woods, it lies to the eastern side of the A16 road, just south of Fotherby. It was presented to the Woodland Trust.

NORFOLK

Bure Marshes Grid reference TG3316. 600 acres. This area of alder woodland may be the best of its kind in Britain. The alder is extensive, occurring sometimes with ash, pedunculate oak and birch, and the shrubs include buckthorn, alder buckthorn, guelder rose and grey sallow. It is possible to see a complete range of successful stages from the original open marsh. It is a National Nature Reserve, part-owned by the Norfolk Naturalists' Trust, and the woodland communities can best be seen from the Hoveton Great Broad nature trail. For details please contact the regional office of the Nature Conservancy Council. Much of the rest of the reserve consists of treacherous and dangerous terrain and access to it is by permit only.

East Wretham Heath Grid reference TL900884. 362 acres. This area of old Scots pine plantations and beech and hornbeam woodland lies within a heathland nature reserve owned and managed by the county trust for nature conservation. It supports a rich bird population, and deer and other fauna. Access is from the warden's office in the north-east corner of the reserve, about 5 miles from Thetford on the A1075. Drove Road, between Langmere and Ringmere, is open to the public, but a permit is needed to enter the reserve (purchase from the warden's office at 10 am or 2 pm).

Wayland Wood Grid reference TL924995. 80 acres. This is a coppice-with-standards wood near Watton, in which oak is the main standard tree species, with some ash and birch. The coppice layer consists mainly of hazel and bird-cherry, with some ash and field maple, dogwood, holly and willow. The ground flora is rich. It is a nature reserve owned and managed by the county trust for nature conservation. Permit needed from the Honorary Warden (who can be contacted through the Norfolk Naturalists' Trust, telephone Norwich 25540). Access is 1 mile south-west of Watton beside the East Dereham–Thetford road (A1075); limited parking on roadside.

NORTHAMPTONSHIRE

Stoke Wood Grid reference SP802864. 26 acres. A remnant of Rockingham Forest, still actively managed as coppice-with-standards woodland, this is one of the last traditionally managed woodlands in the county; coppicing has been continuous, possibly for centuries. It has an oak and ash canopy, an understorey of hazel coppice, and a rich ground flora, including some species which are locally rare. It is a Site of Special Scientific Interest. Situated near Stoke Albany. Access from the B669, opposite the southern end of Bowd Lane Wood (at grid reference SP805864). Owned by the Woodland Trust.

Wood Burcote Grid reference SP690465. 9.5 acres. An old gravel pit near the village of Wood Burcote near Towcester. Used more recently as a council rubbish-tip, it has been filled to its former level and will be planted with trees in coming years. Owned by the Woodland Trust.

NORTHUMBERLAND

Holystone Burn Grid reference NT944020. 55 acres. This area, near Holystone, comprises a wide range of upland woodland and moorland vegetation, with juniper, oak and birch on the valley floor over a rich field layer. Parking on a layby south-west of Holystone village on the road signposted Campville, from where a Forestry Commission road leads into the area.

Holystone North Wood Grid reference NT945028. 38 acres. This area provides a good example of upland sessile-oak woodland. It lies half a mile west of Holystone village on the road signposted to Campville. There is a car park beside the road and access is along a forest trail leading north, through young plantation to the old oakwood.

NORTH YORKSHIRE

Cot Park Wood Grid reference SD7778-7776. 22 acres. This area of subalpine ash woodland is believed to have developed on the limestone pavement as a consequence of cow-grazing pressure. The growth of ash is most dense at the north end of the reserve, though the trees are seldom more than 12 metres high. To the south the tree cover is sparser. Wych-elm and birch are scattered among the ash, together with hazel, rowan, hawthorn and bird-cherry. There is a well-developed community of herbs and bryophytes. It is a National Nature Reserve. Permit to enter obtainable from the regional office of the Nature Conservancy Council.

NOTTINGHAMSHIRE

Hannah Park Wood Grid reference SK590773. 14 acres. Lying on a hill overlooking Worksop, this wood is a remnant of the northern

199

edge of Sherwood Forest. It is an old estate plantation which has developed into high forest, and consists mostly of beech and oak, with some yew; an attractive area of open woodland, popular locally. It is situated along the eastern side of the B6005 road just south of Worksop, and access is possible from that road and from the road on the eastern side of the wood. Ample parking. Owned by the Woodland Trust.

Oldmoor Wood Grid reference SK497428. 38 acres. The largest area of broadleaved woodland remaining in this part of the county, the wood consists of oak, beech and other species, but there is also a small area of pine, planted in 1968 by the National Coal Board, following mining activities. The wood is an old estate plantation which has developed into high forest. It is adjacent to a lake used by local anglers. Less than 5 miles from the centre of Nottingham, close to the Derbyshire border, the wood is clearly visible from the M1 just south of junction 26. Access to it is by a lane crossing over the motorway from the village of Strelley, where parking is available. A fenced right of way runs from the lane to the wood, which is owned by the Woodland Trust.

OXFORDSHIRE

Aston Rowant Woods Grid reference SU741967. 680 acres. This area, on the Oxfordshire–Buckinghamshire border, comprises 6 woods. Grove Wood contains ash, sycamore, beech and elm. Upper Grove Wood contains pedunculate oak, but with much ash and beech, together with coppiced small-leaved lime, gean, hornbeam and hawthorn. Much of Aston Wood is dominated by beech, but there is also ash and gean. Kingston Wood, one of the largest in the area, extends from a plateau down a scarp slope. Beech is dominant on the plateau and much of the slope supports pure stands. Crowell Wood is also dominated by beech, with occasional ash, oak and cherry, and High Wood has a dense beech canopy with occasional ash and oak. A small part of Aston Wood lies within the Aston Rowant National Nature Reserve. To visit parts of the National Nature Reserve away from the public footpath and the nature trail, a permit must be obtained from the regional office of the Nature Conservancy Council. Other woods are owned variously by the National Trust, the Forestry Commission and private individuals, who can advise whether public access is permitted.

Little Garden Wood Grid reference SP353154. 2 acres. This is a young wood, at Ramsden, bordered by a public footpath. Owned by the Woodland Trust.

Trigmoor Wood Grid reference SP256229. 9 acres. This wood, at Kingham, occupies former railway sidings and track. It has been partially planted with conifers and broadleaves by its former owner, and more broadleaves were planted during the winter of 1983. Owned by the Woodland Trust.

Vale Wood Grid reference SP237040. 0.5 acre. A small field at Filkins, near Lechlade, in an area devastated by Dutch elm disease; it has been fenced and planted recently on former open land. Owned by the Woodland Trust.

POWYS

Dolifor Wood Grid reference SN960655. 29 acres. Situated in the Elan Valley, at Llanwrthwl, near Rhayader, this wood was planted fairly recently with a variety of young trees chosen to blend with the local landscape. Access is from the B4518, 1 mile south of Rhayader, from where a lane leads to Dolifor Farm, and a track leads from the farm into the wood. Owned by the Woodland Trust.

Gaer Fawr Wood Grid reference SJ223128. 75 acres. Situated on a steep, saddle-backed hill overlooking the Severn Valley close to the English border, with the banks and ditches of an old hill fort clearly visible at the top of the hill; views over many miles. The wood supports a wide variety of tree and shrub species in many different habitats, including regenerating birch woodland, old coppiced oak, good stands of mixed broadleaved species and, near the top of the hill, occasional groupings of conifers. There is a large open area on the south-western side of the property adding still further to the habitat diversity. There are several good footpaths to the top of the hill, the gentler route following the northern boundary, the more rigorous going straight up from the small car-parking area by the entrance to the site – access is from the minor road on the south-western side of the wood not far from Guilsfield on the B4392. The wood is owned by the Woodland Trust.

Graig Wood Grid reference SJ175085. 8 acres. Situated on a hillside at Castle Caereinion, to the west of Welshpool, this wood consists mainly of sessile-oak standards and coppice, but there are some beech and ash trees around the edges. The wood is beside a lane leading from the A458 Llanfair Caerinion to Welshpool road, and is not far from the B4392 road. Owned by the Woodland Trust.

Nant Irfon Grid reference SN8454. 350 acres. This reserve comprises upland grassland, rocky outcrops and hanging sessile oakwoods on the steep western side of the Irfon valley. The altitude ranges from 950 to 1,250ft. Coedydd Hen-Nant and Digydd are intersected by deep narrow stream gorges and are of a variable structure, containing sessile oak, some rowan, downy birch, hazel and ash, together with a little hawthorn and beech. During the last twenty years some areas have been fenced against grazing stock and set aside for the experimental planting of oak and to encourage natural regeneration. A permit is required to enter this National Nature Reserve, obtainable from the regional office of the Nature Conservancy Council.

Penmoelallt Grid reference S00109. 17 acres. This strip of mixed deciduous woodland represents a type now rare in Wales. It grows on Carboniferous limestone, and on the limestone scree areas the dominant tree is ash, with wych-elm and rowan. At the southern end, where the trees grow on deep clay, the species are more mixed, being dominated by pedunculate oak, with ash, elm, rowan, silver birch and a little small-leaved lime and hazel. The woodland is a Forest Nature Reserve and belongs to the Forestry Commission.

SHROPSHIRE

Workhouse Coppice Grid reference SJ667028. 13.5 acres. A mature oak woodland, rich in wildlife, overlooking the Severn Gorge above Ironbridge, where the Industrial Revolution began. At one time the coppice supplied the factories; today it is no less important as an amenity. A public footpath crosses the wood and access may also be gained from a small road at the southern end. Owned by the Woodland Trust.

SOMERSET

Bickenhall Old Churchyard Grid reference ST286197. 0.5 acre. An old churchyard, containing a massive ancient yew tree, that has been deconsecrated and will be planted with trees, leaving unplanted some areas containing interesting grassland flowers. The churchyard is owned by the Woodland Trust.

Coney Wood Grid reference ST692389. 3 acres. This wood, at Batcombe near Shepton Mallet, is owned by the Woodland Trust.

Couzens Wood Grid reference ST681351. 1 acre. A new wood, near Bruton, planted beside an existing crescent of beech trees. Owned by the Woodland Trust but not open to the public.

Ebbor Gorge Grid reference ST5248. 110 acres. This area of mature woodland, dominated by ash and pedunculate oak, lies on the south-west-facing slope of the Mendips, on Carboniferous limestone, and the area contains caves of palaeontological interest. The dominant trees are associated with wych-elm, beech and a few hornbeam, and the rich understorey contains field maple, dogwood, hazel, spindle, holly, buckthorn, small-leaved lime and wayfaring tree. The scrub is a feature of the area and there is a rich ground flora. The wood forms part of the Mendip Woodlands National Nature Reserve. Visitors are welcome to use the marked paths and a permit to visit other areas or to carry out research is obtainable from the regional office of the Nature Conservancy Council.

North Lodge Copse Grid reference ST397123. 1.32 acres. A small roadside copse of mixed trees, situated on the eastern side of the road running from Dinnington to the A30. Owned by the Woodland Trust.

Rodney Stoke Grid reference ST4950. 86 acres. This area of varied ash woodland also contains oak, lime and elm. Field maple, wych-elm and whitebeam are present, but less common, together with crab-apple, blackthorn, hawthorn, buckthorn, willows and way-faring tree. National Nature Reserve. Entry permits obtainable from the regional office of the Nature Conservancy Council.

Searts Copse Grid reference ST671302. 0.84 acre. Although small, this area of woodland at Shepton Montague is ecologically im-portant. It contains several large oaks, a hazel shrub layer, and a wet area. Owned by the Woodland Trust.

STAFFORDSHIRE

Himley Plantation Grid reference SO870914. 59 acres. On the western edge of the urban West Midlands, at Wombourne, this wood borders a disused railway line managed by the District Council as a Country Park. The wood contains alder, birch, mature oak, beech and Scots pine. It is an old estate plantation which has developed into high forest. Access is from a car park on the eastern side of the wood. From Himley village take the Swindon road and then turn right immediately after the old railway bridge. The wood is owned by the Woodland Trust.

STRATHCLYDE AND CENTRAL

Loch Lomond Grid reference NS4080. 230 acres. The woodland forms part of the 1,028 acre Loch Lomond National Nature Reserve. All the reserve islands lying to the south-eastern end of the loch are thickly wooded and are mainly dominated by oak with birch, hazel and alder in mixture. The woods on the mainland part of the reserve around the mouth of the Endrick Water have been more recently managed, but again have oak and birch with alder and willow in the wetter areas. Access to the main island of Inchcailloch can be easily arranged at the local boatyard at Balmaha. Further information about visits can be obtained from the regional office of the Nature Conservancy Council.

SUFFOLK

Armstrong's Wood Grid reference TL965638. 4.5 acres. Just off the A45 road, to the east of St Andrew's Church in the village of Tostock, this long, narrow wood has suffered badly from Dutch elm disease. Some of the dead trees have been left to provide deadwood habitat for birds, invertebrates and fungi; others have been replaced. Owned by the Woodland Trust. Access is from the road running from Tostock to the A1088 road.

Groton Wood Grid reference TL977432. 50 acres. The northern part of this area has probably been woodland since prehistoric times and it contains the finest stand in Suffolk of coppiced small-leaved lime. The larger, southern part is secondary woodland of varying composition, but the boundary and field banks of the medieval wood remain. In addition to the lime there is oak, ash, birch, field maple, aspen and cherry, with a varied ground flora. The wood is a nature reserve owned and managed by the Suffolk Trust for Nature Conservation. It lies near Groton and access is by a gate in the south-western corner, 2 miles north-east of Boxford and 2 miles south-west of Kersey.

Porter's Wood Grid reference TM264483. 8 acres. Known formerly as Tempe Wood, this wood consists of high oak and beech forest, and also contains many flowering plants, including ramsons or wild garlic (*Allium ursinum*), which fills the wood with its smell. The wood is to the south of Woodbridge, overlooking the Deben estuary, within the Suffolk Coast and Heaths Area of Outstanding Natural Beauty. Access is from a public footpath which leaves the B1438 road at grid reference TM263493 and runs along the western edge of the wood. Owned by the Woodland Trust.

SURREY

Chiphouse Wood Grid reference TQ260570. 20 acres. Situated beside railway land in Chipstead, not far from the B2032 road, 12 acres of this area consist of oak woodland and 8 acres have been planted recently on what was ploughed land. The aim of the planting is to link belts of existing woodland, while leaving wide, grassy glades and rides for the benefit of walkers and wildlife. The older woodland used to be managed as coppice-with-standards of oak and ash above hazel, but it is not being coppiced at present. Access is at either end of the wood and there are several footpaths through it. Owned by the Woodland Trust.

Glover's Wood Grid reference TQ230410. 63 acres. This area of woodland, at Charlwood, is owned by the Woodland Trust and forms part of a larger woodland area which is partly ancient and partly more recent, and which in the past has been coppiced extensively. The species include wych-elm, small-leaved lime and wild service, and there is a rich ground flora. Within the area owned by the Trust is a sphagnum bog. The wood is a Grade II Site of Special Scientific Interest and is crossed by several footpaths. Access to these is from the south-west side of Charlwood.

Nower Wood Grid reference TQ193456. 81 acres. A prominent hilltop feature near Headley, lying on an east-west ridge rising to more than 600ft with steeply sloping flanks and many dells. This wood is dominated by sweet chestnut and oak, together with other native species, with a rich ground flora and fauna. It is an educational nature reserve owned and managed by the county trust for nature conservation. It is open to the public on the first Sunday in each month from April to October inclusive. There is a locked car park on the north side of the Leatherhead–Headley road (B2033) at TQ193546; the keys can be obtained from the keyholder, whose name and address are displayed on a noticeboard in the park.

The Prestige Wood, Hammond's Copse Grid reference TQ213442. 73 acres. At Newdigate, part of the area is a typical remnant of local ancient woodland, containing a predominance of hazel coppice under oak, with a rich and varied flora. The rest of the woodland was cleared and replanted during the last decade, but many of the planted conifers failed and there is vigorous regeneration of broadleaved species native to the site, so that in twenty or thirty years the area should have recovered fully. Owned by the Woodland Trust.

SUSSEX

Beechland Wood Grid reference TQ414205. 1.9 acres. This wood consists of a recently planted mixture of native trees which will augment an existing area of oak woodland. It is situated in a small valley to the south of the village of Newick, and access is by path either from the road to the south of the wood or from the village. Owned by the Woodland Trust.

Brock Wood Grid reference TQ644250. 12 acres. This wood contains oak, hazel and other species. It used to be managed as coppice-with-standards, hazel being coppiced beneath oak. There are plans to reintroduce coppicing. It is situated at Burwash Common in the High Weald Area of Outstanding Natural Beauty. Owned by the Woodland Trust.

Guestling Wood Grid reference TQ863148. 26 acres. This wood forms the northern part of a larger area of woodland within the High Weald Area of Outstanding Natural Beauty. It was formerly managed as sweet-chestnut coppice-with-standards. This manage-ment has been retained in part of the wood, but elsewhere the woodland will be allowed to develop naturally to improve its value as a wildlife habitat. Situated near Hastings, and affords views over the valley of the River Brede. Owned by the Woodland Trust.

Kiln Wood Grid reference TQ527203. 9 acres. This is a fine oak wood with an adjacent area of rough pasture. It contains hornbeam, sweet chestnut and hazel coppice, with scattered trees of birch, holly and willow. Situated at Blackboys, near Uckfield. Owned by the Woodland Trust.

Kingley Vale Grid reference SU824088. 361 acres. This yew wood-land in West Sussex is said to be the best in Europe: yew dominates south-facing steep chalk slopes, with oak growing over plateau and coombe rock in the valley bottom, the yew being the more extensive. There are about 20,000 yew trees, some of them 500 years old. Elsewhere in the wood are ash, whitebeam, holly, hawthorn and blackthorn. This is a National Nature Reserve, much of it open to the public; most is owned by the Nature Conservancy Council.

TAYSIDE

Black Wood of Rannoch Grid reference NN5756. 2,416 acres. This wood, lying on the slopes to the south of Loch Rannoch in Perthshire, is composed mainly of Caledonian Scots pine, with some birch, rowan, alder and a little oak, and willow in wetter places. The wood is famous among entomologists. It is a Forest Nature Reserve, owned by the Forestry Commission. As deer control and game shooting take place, it is advisable to inform the local Forestry Commission supervisor at Kinloch Rannoch before entering the area.

WEST YORKSHIRE

Hetchell Wood Grid reference SE380422. 29 acres. This wood, at Bardsey-cum-Rigton, is on a gritstone escarpment capped by magnesian limestone which is exposed in quarries that may date from Roman times. There is alder swamp and marsh on the lower ground, acid oakwood on drier slopes, and near the top of the slopes are hawthorn thickets with elm and ash. The ground flora is rich and the wood is noted for its insect population. It is a nature reserve managed by the county trust for nature conservation. Access is from Thorner, between the Leeds–York (A64) and Leeds–Wetherby (A58) roads, along the Bardsey road.

WILTSHIRE

Clanger Wood Grid reference ST873538. 105 acres. Former broad-leaved woodland, at Heywood near Westbury, that has been replanted with a mixture of coniferous species, among which blocks of the original oak woodland remain. Renowned for its wildlife, particularly birds and butterflies and spring flowers. There is a wide, open ride running the length of the wood from the entrance on the A350. Parking is limited and visitors are asked not to block the gate. Owned by the Woodland Trust.

Colerne Park
Monks Wood Grid reference ST837727. 111 acres. Much of this

woodland was formerly dominated by wych-elm, many of which have been affected by Dutch elm disease. The dead wood is being cleared and extensive regeneration of the elm is now occurring. Formerly managed as coppice-with-standards, wych-elm being one of the main coppice species, the wood also contains oak and ash woodland. There is a wide variety of flowering herbs, including lily of the valley (*Convallaria majalis*) and two species of Solomon's seal (*Polygonatum*). A small stream runs along the eastern boundary. The wood lies within the Cotswold Area of Outstanding Natural Beauty and much of it is a Grade II Site of Special Scientific Interest. There is the site of a Roman building in Colerne Park. Access to Monks Wood is by a specially negotiated right of way. The woods are close to junctions 16 and 17 of the M4 motorway at Slaughterford, near Chippenham, and together with the field partly separating them are owned by the Woodland Trust.

Tanner's Wood Grid reference SU033373. 2.5 acres. Devastated by Dutch elm disease, this wood consists of two small areas which are being replanted. They lie within the Cranborne Chase and West Wiltshire Downs Area of Outstanding Natural Beauty, in the Wylye Valley, and are owned by the Woodland Trust.

Yatesbury Beeches Grid reference SU060714. 1 acre. This wood consists of a line of beeches bordering the only road into the village of Yatesbury, near Avebury, within the North Wessex Downs Area of Outstanding Natural Beauty. Some trees which had become dangerous have been removed and new beeches planted to replace them. Owned by the Woodland Trust.

Glossary

Allerød The last interstadial in the Devensian, named after the site in Denmark whose fossil pollen record provided the first clear evidence of it. It lasted from about 18,000 to about 12,000 years ago and was followed by a brief return to colder conditions.

ancient woodland An area of both primary and secondary woodland that is known to have been in existence before about 1600. Before that date planting by humans rarely led to the development of secondary woodland and therefore such secondary woodland may be assumed to result from natural regeneration.

ascomycetes *See* fungus

Atlantic Period An episode of warm weather, which in Britain lasted from about 7,500 to 5,000 years ago.

basidiomycetes *See* fungus

bolling The stump of a pollarded tree from which grow the shoots that provide the crop.

broadleaved woodland Woodland in which broadleaved tree species comprise at least 80 per cent of the total number of trees.

conifer woodland Woodland in which coniferous tree species comprise at least 80 per cent of the total number of trees.

coppice 1 (verb) a: To fell a tree by cutting it close to the ground in order to allow shoots to grow from the stump. The shoots are harvested to provide stakes, poles, etc. b: To manage an area of woodland in this way. c: To erect a fence around an area of coppiced woodland. 2 (noun): A tree which has been coppiced, or area of woodland containing such trees.

coppice-with-standards A system of woodland management in which most trees are coppiced but selected individuals are allowed to grow to their full (standard) size, being felled when they are mature to provide large timber.

Devensian The last glacial episode (ice age), lasting for about 40,000–60,000 years, during which southern England was ice-covered for about 3,000 years and northern England for about 15,000. It ended about 10,000 years ago.

Dryas, Older and Younger Two periods during the Allerød interstadial when conditions were cooler, both of them marked by the presence of mountain avens (*Dryas octopetala*), a low, creeping shrub typical of Arctic or Alpine conditions. The temporary return of colder climatic conditions during the Younger *Dryas* may have reduced the wooded area in Britain greatly, and the forests may have disappeared.

epiphyte A plant which grows on another, using its host only for support and taking no nutrients from it. It does no harm to the host.

Flandrian The present interglacial period, following the Devensian glaciation, which began about 10,000 years ago.

forest From the Latin *foris*, outside. 1 (noun) a: An area of land covered with trees, often trees that have been planted by humans. b: Land which lay beyond the cultivated and enclosed farm land and was unfenced; it might or might not be covered with trees. c: An area of land whose use was subject to 'forest law', relating mainly to game. Much of the forest which was once tree-covered has since been cleared, but the word 'forest' may be retained in the name, eg Dartmoor Forest, Sherwood Forest. 2 (verb): To plant with trees.

fruiting body The visible part of many fungi, which appears above the surface of the soil or other material in which the fungus grows. It is the reproductive organ, which produces and then releases the spores, and appears only briefly.

fungus A member of the taxonomic kingdom Mycota, differing from a plant (kingdom Metaphyta) in that it cannot synthesise nutrients from inorganic compounds. Most fungi produce minute fruiting bodies, which are their visible parts. Those which are large and often colourful belong to two major divisions: the ascomycetes, which include truffles, morels and many moulds, and the basidiomycetes which include the mushrooms and toadstools, puffballs, stinkhorns, boletes and earth stars, as well as a number of plant parasites.

high forest Woodland comprising single-stemmed trees with no coppice present, managed sustainably on long rotations for the production of mature timber.

horizon A clearly defined layer revealed by a cross-section cut vertically through a soil. Each horizon has its own characteristics, and it is by their horizons that soils are classified taxonomically.

interglacial A prolonged warm period between two periods of glaciation.

interstadial A warmer period during a glaciation in which the glaciers retreat partially. Botanically, temperatures still remain too low, or the period is too short, to permit the establishment of the vegetation pattern that would develop during a full interglacial.

isostasy Literally 'equal standing', a concept which holds that above a certain level in the earth, called the 'level of compensation', any column of material up to the surface will have the same mass as any other column, provided both have the same cross-sectional area. If one column is shorter than another, because at that point the crust is thinner, then it will be made from denser rock. When ice forms thickly on the surface, the underlying rocks cannot be compressed, but they are depressed and the isostatic balance is disturbed. When the ice melts, the rocks rise, and equilibrium is restored.

level of compensation *See* isostasy

lichen An organism formed from the symbiotic partnership of an alga and a fungus, the fungus usually determining the overall appearance of the lichen. The alga manufactures carbohydrates by photosynthesis, and nourishes the fungus. Lichens are now considered to be fungi with an unusual way of obtaining the nutrients they need.

mycelium The main part of the body of a fungus, consisting of a fine network of filaments lying within the soil or other material in which the fungus grows.

naturalised Applied to species that have been introduced by humans, but which have become established and now spread by their own means.

natural woodland Woodland composed wholly of trees which have not been planted by humans, and which is entirely unmanaged.

phytosociology The study of plant communities as societies within which species interact, the development and structure of such communities, their classification and their relationships with the wider environment.

plant association A basic unit of ecological classification, comprising 1: a group of areas all of which are dominated by the same species; 2: according to the phytosociological method, areas in which a particular group of species occurs very commonly.

pollard 1: (verb) To fell a tree by cutting it about 8 to 12ft above ground level in order to allow shoots to grow from the stump (bolling). The shoots are cropped. 2: (noun) A tree so managed.

primary woodland Woodland occupying a site that is known to have been wooded continuously throughout the historical period, and by implication since the last glaciation.

secondary woodland Woodland resulting from natural succession or the planting of unwooded land that occupies a site that has not been wooded continuously throughout the historical period.

semi-natural woodland Woodland comprising mainly native species which appear not to have been planted, but which has been managed at some period during its history. Semi-natural woodland may be of secondary origin.

spinney An area of woodland in which the dominant species are, or were, thorns (blackthorn, hawthorn, etc).

taxonomy The scientific classification of organisms and groups of organisms arranged in hierarchies. Each group, eg family, within a hierarchy is a taxon (pl taxa). A person specialising in such classification is a taxonomist.

timber The produce of tree-trunks in pieces large enough to be used as beams in construction or sawn into planks.

wildwood The original, primeval vegetation pattern that covered most of Britain by the end of the Atlantic Period, about 5,000 years ago; it was the vegetation into which the first human migrants moved.

wood 1: A small area in which trees are the dominant plants. 2: The produce of small trees or branches, not large enough to be classed as timber.

woodland A tree-covered area, usually smaller than a forest.

wood-pasture Open woodland in which livestock graze.

Chronologies

The Late and Post-Pleistocene in Britain
(Dates by radiocarbon dating)

Date (years ago)	Period	Climate	Vegetation
14,000	Late Weichselian:		
	Lower Dryas	cold	least willow
12,000	Allerød	milder	birch
	Upper Dryas	cold	least willow
10,000	Flandrian:		
	Pre-Boreal	dry	birch–pine
	Boreal	dry	hazel–birch–pine
8,000	Boreal	dry	hazel–pine
7,000	Atlantic	dry	alder–oak–elm–lime
5,000	Sub-Boreal	dry	alder–oak–lime (elm decline)
3,000	Sub-Atlantic	rapid deterioration	alder–birch–oak–beech
1,000		warm	alder–birch–oak–beech

British Archaeology

Date (years ago)	Culture	Forest cover
14,000	Upper Palaeolithic	grass, sedge and open vegetation
12,000	Upper Palaeolithic	grass, sedge and open vegetation
10,000	Protomaglemosian	forest maximum
8,000	Mesolithic	forest maximum
5,000	Neolithic	forest clearance begins
4,000	Bronze Age	forest clearance
3,000	Iron Age	forest clearance
2,000	Romano-British	forest clearance
	Anglo-Saxon	forest clearance
1,000	Norman	forest clearance

Both tables based on Godwin, H. *History of the British Flora*, 2nd ed. (Cambridge Univ Press, 1975).

Further Reading

Allaby, M. *The Changing Uplands.* (Countryside Commission, HMSO, London, 1983)

Beckett, K. and G. *Planting Native Trees and Shrubs.* (Jarrold Colour Publications, Norwich, 1979)

Bellamy, D. *Discovering the Countryside: Woodland Walks.* (Hamlyn Publishing Group Ltd, Feltham, Middx, 1982)

van den Brink, F. H. *A Field Guide to the Mammals of Britain and Europe*, 5th ed. (Wm Collins Sons & Co Ltd., London, 1977)

Clapham, A. R., Tutin, T. G. and Warburg, E. F. *Flora of the British Isles*, 2nd ed. (Cambridge Univ Press, 1962)

The Conservation and Development Programme for the UK Sponsored by the World Wildlife Fund, Nature Conservancy Council, Countryside Commission, Countryside Commission for Scotland, Royal Society of Arts, Council for Environmental Conservation. (Kogan Page, London, 1983)

Corbet, G. B. *Finding and Identifying Mammals in Britain.* (British Museum (Natural History), London, 1975)

Corbet, G. B. and Southern, H. N. *The Handbook of British Mammals*, 2nd ed. (Blackwell Scientific Publications, Oxford, 1977)

Cousens, J. *An Introduction to Woodland Ecology.* (Oliver & Boyd, Edinburgh, 1974)

Dickinson, C. and Lucas, J. *The Encyclopaedia of Mushrooms.* (Orbis Publishing, London, 1979)

Duncan, U.K. *Introduction to British Lichens.* (T. Buncle & Co, Arbroath, 1970. Available from Richmond Publishing Co, Ltd, Orchard Road, Richmond, Surrey TW9 4PD)

Edlin, H. L. *British Woodland Trees*, 2nd ed. (B. T. Batsford Ltd, London, 1945)

Edlin, H. L. *Trees, Woods and Man*, 3rd ed. New Naturalist Series. (Wm Collins Sons & Co, Ltd, London, 1970)

Evans, J. G. *The Environment of Early Man in the British Isles.* (Paul Elek Ltd, London, 1975)

Fleure, H. J. and Davies, M. *A Natural History of Man in Britain*,

Fontana New Naturalist series. (Wm Collins Sons & Co, Ltd, London, 1971)

Forestry Commission *Know Your Conifers*, 2nd ed. Forestry Commission Booklet 15. (HMSO, London, 1970)

Forestry Commission *Know Your Broadleaves*. Forestry Commission Booklet 20. (HMSO, London, 1968, reprinted with amendments 1975)

Godwin, H. *History of the British Flora*, 2nd ed. (Cambridge Univ Press, 1975)

Havins, P. J. N. *The Forests of England*. (Robert Hale & Co, London, 1976)

Heywood, V. H. (consultant editor) *Flowering Plants of the World*. (Oxford Univ Press, 1978)

Hora, B. (consultant editor) *The Oxford Encyclopaedia of Trees of the World*. (Oxford Univ Press, 1981)

Jeffrey, C. *An Introduction to Plant Taxonomy*, 2nd ed. (Cambridge Univ Press, 1982)

Kibby, G. *Mushrooms and Toadstools, a Field Guide*. (Oxford Univ Press, 1979)

Lever, C. *The Naturalised Animals of the British Isles*. (Hutchinson & Co, Ltd, London, 1977)

Mabey, R. *Plants With a Purpose*. (Wm Collins Sons & Co, Ltd, London, 1977)

Mabey, R. *The Common Ground*. (Hutchinson & Co, Ltd, London, 1980)

Pennington, W. *The History of British Vegetation*, 2nd ed. (English Univ, Press Ltd, London, 1974)

Phillips, R. *Trees in Britain, Europe and North America*. (Pan Books Ltd, London, 1978)

Pollard, E., Hooper, M. D., and Moore, N. W. *Hedges*. New Naturalist series. (Wm Collins Sons & Co, Ltd, London, 1974)

Rackham, O. *Trees and Woodland in the British Landscape*. (J. M. Dent & Sons Ltd, London, 1976)

Rackham, O. *Ancient Woodland: Its History, Vegetation and Usage in England*. (Edward Arnold Ltd, London, 1980)

Rose, F. *The Wild Flower Key*. (Frederick Warne & Co, Ltd, London, 1981)

Step, E. *Wayside and Woodland Trees*. (Frederick Warne & Co, Ltd, London, 1940)

Tansley, A. G. *Introduction to Plant Ecology*, (George Allen & Unwin Ltd, London, 1946)

Taylor, C. *Fields in the English Landscape*. (J. M. Dent & Sons Ltd, London, 1975)

Thomas, G. S. *Trees in the Landscape*. (Jonathan Cape Ltd, London, 1983)

West, R. G. *Pleistocene Geology and Biology*, 2nd ed. (Longman Group Ltd, London, 1977)

Wilkinson, G. *Epitaph for the Elm*. (Hutchinson Publishing Group, London, 1978)

Index

NR = Nature Reserve; NNR = National Nature Reserve

217